Games For Success

Developing Children's Character Through Recreational Play

D1563245

Foreword by
Warren Fraleigh

Steven A. Henkel

University Press of America, Inc.
Lanham • New York • London

Copyright © 1995 by
University Press of America,® Inc.
4720 Boston Way
Lanham, Maryland 20706

3 Henrietta Street
London, WC2E 8LU England

Library of Congress Cataloging-in-Publication Data

Henkel, Steven Alan.
Games for success : developing children's character through
recreational play / Steven A. Henkel ; foreword by Warren Fraleigh.
p.   cm.
Includes biblliographical references and index.
1. Games--Social aspects. 2. Self-esteem in children. 3. Personality
development. 4. Success--Psychological aspects. I. Title.
GV1201.38.H46   1995   790.1'922--dc20   95-9579 CIP

ISBN 0-7618-0009-3 (pbk: alk ppr)

⊖™ The paper used in this publication meets the minimum
requirements of American National Standard for Information
Sciences—Permanence of Paper for Printed Library Materials,
ANSI Z39.48—1984

Dedication

APPRECIATE KIDS WHO ARE DIFFERENT,

WHO TRY, BUT FLOUNDER IN GAMES.

THEY MISS A BIG PASS,

THEN RUN OUT OF GAS,

AND MAKE NO HALLS OF FAME.

IF ONLY KIDS COULD BE DIFFERENT,

AND STILL SUCCEED IN GAMES,

THEY'D TRY EVEN MORE

WHATEVER THE SCORE,

AND LEARN TO VALUE THEIR NAMES.

This book is dedicated to the children who are different--children who fail in traditional games--children who could succeed if someone would redefine success--children who could learn to value themselves for who they are in God's eyes, instead of for what they can do.

Contents

Foreword

Play in games is a major element in the engagement of children
with their world. Children's game playing provides the direct
experiences of interacting with others and the environment,
socialization into dominant values and taboos, self expression, and the
acquisition of some sense of self. Indeed, writer Albert Camus is
credited with saying that everything he learned about ethics he learned
by playing sport. The impact of children's game playing may be
positive or negative with respect to values.

Dr. Henkel is fully aware of the developmental impact of children's
games. He recognizes that they are necessarily value-laden enterprises,
that they operate to orient, to teach, to reinforce, or to examine both
desirable or undesirable values. Whether or not games are adult
organized or child initiated, engagement in them will entail experiences
of values. Accordingly, he helps us to appreciate that whenever adults
organize children's games they will have some influence on the
development of values. Thus, the question is not whether leaders of
games should consciously plan for value content--it is there--but what
values do they wish to influence and how may they do so? This latter
question deserves careful attention and clear-cut answers, particularly
with reference to moral values.

In this book Professor Henkel establishes a rationale which enables
adult leaders to systematically structure games to enhance the
acquisition of positive values among elementary and middle school age
children. He shows that it is both the responsibility and the
opportunity for adults to organize game experiences wherein widespread
success by participants occurs, and values such as self-esteem, honesty
and fairness are maximized.

Dr. Henkel's recommendations for the use of games to inculcate
positive, humane values comes at a time when the opposite is prevalent
in adult sport on television. Children too often view negative, anti-
social actions such as hostility, gratuitous violence, self-centered
boasting, and intentional rules violations in contemporary sport. It is
possible that this negative modeling by adult sports "heroes" impacts
deleteriously on children's understanding of "appropriate" behavior in

game situations. Indeed, what is the message sent to the social structure of children's games when rules are made in a high school football league which prohibit opponents from shaking hands following a game? Or what is the significance of the current NCAA intercollegiate wrestling rules which call the act of a wrestler shaking the hand of the official "unethical behavior"? The point is, that unless leaders of children's games examine and structure game experiences so as to emphasize positive values, the adult sports world may structure these same experiences into negative value consequences.

Steve Henkel provides clear, systematic and consistent instruction on how children's games may become sources for the development of positive values. While he places emphasis on values compatible with Christian biblical sources, it is likely that many of these same values are appropriate apart from religious connections, for secular situations. This is to say that the ways of structuring experiences in children's games could be useful to any adult leader of games.

Warren P. Fraleigh, Professor
Department of Sport and Physical
    Education
State University of New York
College at Brockport
January, 1995

Preface

Another Side of Games

..."We now return to our regularly scheduled traditional competitive game, where *Effort* is attempting to become 'King of the Mountain'...There he goes, fans! Let's all watch *Effort* as he tries to scale that wall of snow. In order to be 'King of the Mountain' he must make it to the top. Many others have made it, so we can expect the same from him...

...It looks like *Effort* is trying the right side first...He's making some progress, though slower than the others...He'll soon be to the first obstacle. It's going to be difficult getting around that large snow bank. He'll need to grip tightly...There's one hand hold...and another...I think he made it...Yes! Now on to the next snow bank...He's leaning into the hill...Oh no! He's been pushed down the side by *Aggressive*! I'm sure he won't let that discourage him. He can withstand a couple of bumps...

...Now *Effort* is going to try the left side...He's climbing diagonally to the outside. He'll have to get over a large dip in the snow bank...Here comes the jump...*Effort* is taking to the air...It's not a very high take-off. He'll need to sail far in order to have a chance...Whoops, one leg did not make it. I believe that *Rut* has trapped his leg. If he can just pull it out he might be able to...Yes! The leg is free, but now he's rolling down the hill out of control--a few more bruises for the lad, but nothing he can't handle...

...*Effort* is moving up once again. If only he can make it to the top...I hope he sees the icy spot coming up. This will be a key turning point if he can make it over this obstacle. Maybe *Effort* can gain some confidence for the remainder of the climb...He's trying to dig in his boot...definitely showing a lot of determination...He's part way over the ice...Now *Effort* is reaching with the other foot...just a little farther...Oh no! Down he goes again. I'm afraid *Slick* has gotten the best of him this time. Wow, does he look discouraged. I'm not sure how much longer *Effort* can go on..."

How much longer do you think a child like *Effort* can endure failure? Perhaps not very long. And if a child can endure failure, at what cost? The 'King of the Mountain' metaphor could reflect a child's experience in a variety of physical activities, but particularly the experience of unsuccessful children in traditional competitive games. Children try to meet the challenge at hand, whether it be catching a ball or running to a base. They make some progress, but are seldom successful because they cannot perform as well as the expectation. Someone usually "shoves them back down the mountain."

So, unsuccessful children begin the climb again and the cycle repeats itself. The children make it around one obstacle and perhaps, a second. They may overcome some physical bumps and emotional bruises for awhile, but again success is out of view. Why is success so elusive? It is unattainable because the children are looking through a foggy lens. No one taught them to view success as doing their best first of all, and as overcoming one obstacle at a time second of all. Instead, many children are taught that success is achieved by "getting all the way to the top." Children who fail over and over have wounded self-esteems and eventually give up.

In the metaphor, the child tried scaling the right and left sides of the mountain. Is there another side of the mountain--another side of games in general, where all children can be successful? Indeed there is and children need help to climb it. Some educators believe forsaking competition altogether is necessary to eliminate widespread failure. I disagree. Instead, children can experience "games for success" through three avenues: alternative competitive games, cooperative games, and independent games.

Part I of the book reveals common elements of games, as well as challenges associated with the different game avenues. Each of the challenges may be overcome by making choices that include, rather than exclude, children. Being included is critical to the development of a child's self-esteem.

Part II provides game leaders with actual games for success to use in a variety of educational settings with elementary and middle school age children. Games will benefit leaders and children not only in schools, but also in home schools, churches, camps and other community settings. Ideas include suggestions for promoting character development through game play. With so many negative role models in the sports media, the need for promoting positive values has never been more acute. Although the values are universal and applicable to any setting, this book recognizes the Bible as the source of the values because it is the inspired, infallible Word of God. Therefore, the book is especially helpful for leaders in Christian education programs, including those who train leaders in Christian higher education. Leaders are encouraged to try the games provided, and to use the ideas to generate more games of their own. For people with limited experience leading recreational activities, Part II includes a chapter on selected "how to's" of administrating games.

Throughout the book success is defined as "doing one's best in accomplishing a task." Whether playing games, writing a poem, or washing dishes, doing one's best requires having a pure motive (1 Samuel 17:46; Proverbs 16:3), appropriating skill (Ecclesiastes 10:10), and valuing help from others (Proverbs 15:22). A given task may or may not actually require help from others, and it may or may not involve an opponent. Although success requires appropriating skill, it also involves divine intervention or oversight. A person needs to seek the Lord (1 Samuel 14:47; 2 Chronicles 26:5) and recognize that His grace makes task completion possible. Otherwise, a person's efforts are in vain (Psalm 127:1-2).

Acknowledgments

I appreciate the assistance of dear friends and family in writing this book. The late Neal Earls helped me think critically about what activities are and are not appropriate for children. Neal also introduced me to the work of Terry Orlick and David and Roger Johnson during graduate school. My exposure to their work provided many of the ideas on which this book is based.

Rozell Henkel, Dan Midura, John Pamperin and Emily Willecke reviewed drafts of the book, and suggested points of clarity or elaboration that are now incorporated into the text. Warren Fraleigh wrote the Foreword for the book, which situates ideas in a larger social and moral context. Adam Turner drew unique sketches of games with grant money provided by the Bethel College Alumni Board. Thanks to each of you for sharing your expertise.

This book could not have been written without the patience and support of my family. They sacrificed a corner of the basement during a six-month sabbatical, and countless hours thereafter. Thank you especially, Vicki, for your proof reading and your encouragement when my progress was slow.

A final word of thanks goes to the many children who endured the piloting of games. Every game did not work the first time. Some games evolved because children were willing to try something new, and because they were patient when I made adjustments "on the spot." Let this be an encouragement to readers who make up your own games.

Part I Challenges and Choices

Games present challenges to leaders. Leaders need to select games for children from a vast assortment available. Children may or may not succeed in a game because they range so much in developmental level and in skills acquired. Even when a game is appropriately chosen, leaders have the challenge of understanding all the elements involved and how to explain them to children. Each of these challenges is addressed in Part I.

In chapter 1 the nature of a game is closely examined. Understanding general aspects of play and specific game elements helps leaders match a game with a particular purpose or reason for playing. Leaders will also gain a better understanding of the challenges associated with different social structures within games.

Chapter 2 considers the relationship of social structure and other elements to self-esteem. The chapter answers questions such as, "What are the building blocks of self-esteem"? and "How can I include all children in a game"? Leaders are presented with choices for changing games to meet the needs of children of all ability levels. In the case of competitive games, the choices have to do with monitoring the way people compete and the extent of their competitiveness. This is the subject of chapter 3.

Chapter 1

Nature of a Game

Recreational games provide a primary way for children to interact with, and learn from, their world. Games offer opportunities to practice motor skills, learn social values, and shape personal identity. In addition to a game's outcomes, the nature of a game may be defined by describing what people do during the game--play, and by describing specific elements that comprise a game.

Aspects of Play

Classic works on play suggest some general aspects common to all play forms. These aspects are captured by Huizinga (1955), who describes play in the following manner:

> a free activity standing quite consciously outside 'ordinary' life as being 'not serious,' but at the same time absorbing the player intensely and utterly. It is an activity connected with no material interest, and no profit can be gained by it. It proceeds within its own proper boundaries of time and space...(p.13).

According to Huizinga, play is first of all free, or **voluntary**. A child enters into play by an act of her own free will. Play occurs during leisure time and so may be deferred or suspended at any time. It is not a task to be done by an individual, nor is it imposed on a person by someone else as an obligation or duty. Organized sport, then, does not represent play in its truest sense, since the child's will is bound by commitment to the team.

A second general aspect of play is its nonordinary, or **unreal** nature. It involves removing oneself from normal life. Sometimes removal occurs directly, as in make believe play. The thing or situation being played out does not actually exist in the life of the child. Common play characters of this kind include a pirate or princess. Most of the time removal from normal life is indirect. Even though children do not make believe in typical recreational games, they may remove themselves from normal life in the sense that all other concerns are potentially left behind.

Thirdly, play is **pleasing**, an end in itself. It is entered into for enjoyment. Activities pursued with material gain in mind, such as prizes or trophies, are not considered true play. Although Huizinga acknowledges that material purposes may be accomplished indirectly through play, the intrinsic value of play provides reason enough to participate.

The remaining aspect of play is its **secludedness**. Play forms are bound by limits of space and time. Spatial limitations include the setting and the boundaries. Settings range from a playground to a back yard outdoors, from a gymnasium to a hallway indoors. Sometimes a play space is further limited by boundaries within the setting, such as lines or markers.

The size and shape of boundaries are critical to accomplishing a game's goal(s). A game that emphasizes aerobic fitness, such as *Flag Quest* (p.138), requires a large enough area to spread out players in order to move optimally. By contrast, the game *Dribble Tag* (p.140) is only effective when players are kept in close proximity. Too large a space limits interaction between players. Whatever the setting and/or boundaries, play occurs within a temporary world. Although a game may be repeated frequently, a single occurrence has a definite beginning and is confined to a relatively clear time frame.

Aspects of play described here are helpful in understanding the nature of a game. The aspects are not all encompassing, however, since all games are play, but not all forms of play are games. Therefore, the nature of a game in this book is also characterized by more specific elements.

Elements of a Game

The elements of a game may be described using the "GAMES" acronym. Each of the elements in the acronym contains particular examples that distinguish one game from another:

G = Goals
A = Alignment
M = Movements
E = Equipment
S = Social structure

Goals

The first common element of games is their educational value. While I embrace the intrinsic value of play, this book is written primarily to promote educational ends achieved through play. Children can have fun and learn something too. In a Christian setting, the educational ends include learning and applying biblical principles. Children may fulfill the need to play for its own sake when they are not being guided by adults. The distinction, then, is between guiding and supervising activities. Often children are supervised during recess, at the neighborhood playground, or in their yard. Adult presence may be more for insuring safety, than for initiating meaningful play ideas.

On the other hand, adults are responsible to guide children in their play choices while in the role of an educator. Serving as a guide requires a thorough understanding of alternative goals and how they may be achieved--a challenge to be sure. While the role of an educator is obvious in the school or home school setting, leaders in youth sports and other community programs may also serve primarily as teachers.

So, what kinds of goals may educational game leaders choose besides having fun? Although games in this book are physical in nature, goals extend beyond practicing motor skills or improving fitness. Other goals may be social, intellectual, or even spiritual in nature. Social goals include respecting others or being trustworthy. Intellectual goals include learning particular concepts or solving problems. Examples of more specific goals are provided in chapter 2, in the context of *Baseball*.

Spiritual goals in recreational games are the least common of all goals. Spiritual goals may reinforce general aspects of character and promote the learning of specific biblical facts and principles. Examples of games that address character within a biblical framework are contained in chapter 4.

Alignment

Every game has an alignment, or way that players are arranged spatially. While not exhaustive, Figure 1.1 depicts several examples.

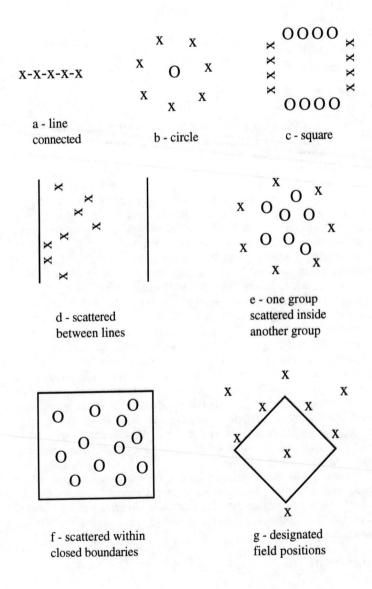

Figure 1.1: Examples of player alignments.

Common examples include geometrical shapes (i.e. Alignments a, b, and c in Figure 1.1). Players within alignments may or may not be connected. Alignment a in the figure illustrates players connected in a chain. Arrangement of players may or may not change during the course of a game. Change does not occur in *Fruit of the Room* (p.97), depicted by Alignment b. Player alignment does change in *Rhythmical Red Light* (p.117), in which people initially stand on one line, then move in scatter arrangement to the other line (i.e. Alignment d). In addition to player alignments changing, more than one alignment may occur simultaneously. For instance, one group of players may be scattered inside another group of players who form a shape (i.e. Alignment e).

Although players may be scattered in no recognizable shape, the boundaries of a game may form a shape around players, as depicted by Alignment f. The final alignment illustrated in Figure 1.1 shows players in designated field positions (i.e. Alignment g). Locations of designated positions are based on the number and experience of players, as well as the motor skills performed.

Movements

Games described in this book involve physical exercise. Exercise may directly target motor skills, and/or may be used to help accomplish other goals. Either way, all "games for success" involve some large muscle movements unlike more sedentary games, such as dressing up in adult clothes or pushing buttons to a video game.

Children use a variety of motor skills or patterns while playing games. Four classifications of motor skills are represented in Table 1.1. Classifications include (a) locomotor patterns, (b) nonlocomotor patterns, (c) object control skills, and (d) sport skills.

Locomotor patterns involve moving the body from place to place, which occurs while galloping or running. Nonlocomotor patterns consist of actions the body does in place, such as bending or stretching. Sport skills are distinguished from object control skills and locomotor patterns based on the complexity of the situation. Games involving object control may require players to throw or strike a ball in a basic sense, whereas games with sport skills might require players to utilize the throw and strike in the form of a pitch or spike, respectively. The latter examples involve precision and accuracy not required of basic skills. Likewise, when a game requires children to perform a long jump for maximum distance, the movement is considered a complex sport skill, rather than a basic locomotor pattern.

Skills utilized in games may be chosen by game leaders or by players. Allowing input from players is one way to match skills to their interests and developmental levels. Another way is to provide alternatives within the same game. Game alternatives and other developmental considerations are discussed in more detail in chapter 2.

Table 1.1

Examples of Motor Skills by Classification

Locomotor patterns		Nonlocomotor patterns	
Galloping	Running	Bending	Stretching
Hopping	Skipping	Curling	Swaying
Jumping	Sliding	Rocking	Turning
Leaping	Walking	Spinning	Twisting
Object control skills		**Sport skills**	
Bouncing	Rolling	Batting	Pitching
Catching	Striking	Bowling	Punting
Collecting	Swinging	Fielding	Serving
Dribbling	Throwing	High jumping	Spiking
Kicking	Tossing	Long jumping	Volleying

Equipment

Equipment may be the most familiar aspect of games. Equipment represents (a) spatial boundaries on the floor or ground, (b) spatial boundaries in the air, (c) items used with patterns of locomotion and nonlocomotion, (d) items used in object control or sport skill tasks, and (e) items worn on the body. Spatial boundaries on the floor or ground are commonly marked with bases, cones, ropes or tape. Markers must be chosen to fit the environmental conditions. In general, indoor markers can be short, lightweight and fewer in number when permanent lines are present. Outdoor markers generally need to be taller, heavier and more plentiful. Markers with these specifications withstand the wind and uneven ground, and increase visibility.

Spatial boundaries in the air include a net, rope or wall. Walls are dangerous boundaries in games, particularly if players advance toward them. Instead, leaders should enforce stringent boundaries inside the walls. A wall can serve as an effective target, however, as long as equipment, rather than players, contact the wall.

A variety of equipment may be used to enhance locomotor and nonlocomotor patterns. With locomotor patterns, equipment serves as a spatial reference point or as an obstacle. In *Chain Tag* (p.130), a hoop or tire serves as a reference point for the tagger to return to intermittently. During *Invent a Course* (p.100), cones, tires and other equipment serve as obstacles for children to go around, over or through. Equipment used with nonlocomotor patterns includes beanbags, hoops, wands and scarves. Equipment may be balanced on the body in different positions (i.e. resting a beanbag on the back while bending over) or manipulated by the body, as in *Loop da Hoop* (p.88).

Items used in object control or sports skill tasks are similar to those used with locomotor and nonlocomotor patterns. Balls and rackets are common examples. Items need to be chosen with safety and the nature of the learning environment in mind. When considering safety, the longer and heavier a racket, the more spacing required between players. The smaller and heavier a ball, the less throwing velocity permitted in a game. With regard to the environment, the windy outdoors requires different object control equipment than a protected gymnasium. A game that utilizes a wiffle ball indoors, may require a tennis ball outdoors.

Items worn on the body consist of flags and pinnies. Velcro flags are preferred for tagging games to clarify who is and who is not tagged. On the other hand, pinnies or jerseys can be more visibly seen in games that distinguish teams.

As with other game elements, flexibility with equipment is key in achieving stated goals. Criteria for determining developmental appropriateness of equipment is discussed in chapter 2.

Social Structure

The social structure of a game involves the number of players or groups of players in a game, as well as the way in which players or groups relate to one another. Game leaders have three choices for relationships among players: competitive, cooperative or independent. A competitive game has been traditionally characterized by mutually exclusive goals--that is, the success of one player or team reduces the success of other players or teams. Competition may occur between two individuals (i.e. *Table Tennis*), within a single group (i.e. *Four Square*), or between two or more groups (i.e. *Volleyball*). Competitive games may also be classified as "zero sum" activities (Brown & Grineski, 1992, p.22), in which there is one winner and one loser (i.e. *Table Tennis*), or "negative sum" activities (Brown & Grineski, 1992, p.22), which result in one winner and more than one loser (i.e. *Four Square*).

In other words, players strive to gain rewards which are in limited supply. Rewards consist of points, prizes or other recognition. Professionals debate whether competition can involve just one individual. In other words, a person could theoretically compete against herself and/or against "the elements." Contests of this kind provide challenge without comparing individuals. Although individual activities are important for rounding out a child's skill development and games participation, the debate is beyond the scope of this book. Since "games for success" intentionally addresses group games, all references to competition involve two or more individuals.

In contrast to a traditional competitive game, a cooperative game is characterized by mutually compatible goals. The success of one player or team contributes to the success of other players or teams. Rewards are not limited because all participants potentially share in obtaining those available. In *Clockwise Four Square* (p.87), rewards consist of cumulative group hits or points. Children cooperate by striking a ball the most number of consecutive times as a group, instead of compete by trying to get others "out." More experienced children can strike the ball with their nondominant hands only and/or hit the ball as many times as possible in a given period of time.

Aspects of competitive and cooperative social structures may be contained in the same game. When the predominant social structure is characterized by competition between different teams, players within the same team may potentially cooperate with one another. Cooperation within competition may also occur when individuals try to defeat one small group (i.e. *Let My People Go*, p.56), or when small groups try to defeat one individual (i.e. *Chain Tag*, p.130).

The least common option for social structure involves independence of players. In other words, the success of one player or team is not related to the success of other players or teams. In *Rhythmical Red Light* (p.117), partners moving from one line to the other line can be in charge of their own destiny. The scoring of one pair does not hinder or help another pair's scoring, as long as leaders utilize both a midline and endline for scoring. Although social contact between players may occur, socialization is incidental in that it is not critical to fulfill predetermined game goals.

The relationship between players in games receives a lot of attention due to peoples' desire to either promote or oppose traditional competition. Some proponents equate play and competition. Most proponents at least defend the status quo by claiming that competition is an unavoidable part of life that children prepare for through experience (Ruben, 1981). Parental support for this claim can be found in good measure (Walsh, 1987):

...it is a good idea to encourage children to participate in some form of physical activity whether it be a team or individual sport with some degree of competitiveness involved. Let's face it, today's world is competitive, and the better prepared our kids are for it, the better chance they have of being successful (p.2).

Proponents further contend that competition provides the best means of being productive and having fun. Winning is viewed as the ultimate goal to achieve. Character development is thought to occur from children's responses to both winning and losing. Winning was given "top billing" at a 1993 Little League banquet. A retired professional baseball player gave the following advice to a room full of coaches:

We need to teach our players to win. That's the only way they walk away happy. When they lose they walk away with long faces and say, 'That umpire was awful', or 'Did you see how the other team cheated?' So they need to learn how to win.

The Little League speaker could have taken his cue from Vince Lombardi, one of the most heralded winners from the 1960's. To set the record straight, though, Lombardi did not say that winning is everything, as the misquotes often attest. Instead, he said that "Winning isn't everything; trying to win is" (Bavolek, 1993, p.2; O'Brian, 1987, p.197). The latter statement emphasizes striving to win, whereas the former idea requires actually winning. Although Lombardi's correct quote is understandable in the professional ranks, neither the correct quote or the misquote has any place in children's games. More children can and will succeed if winning is a peripheral, rather than a primary goal.

Those opposing competition for young children recognize that competing and cooperating are learned behaviors. Some claim that competition has detrimental effects on children's social behavior--that game structure encourages aggression and unfair play. Opponents are also concerned about the effects of competition on future participation due to children's demoralization (Ames, 1984; Robinson, 1989).

The single greatest concern of opponents is the effects of competition on self-esteem. Since traditional competition involves mutually exclusive goals, many children are destined to fail on a regular basis. Apparently, the Little League speaker overlooked inevitable failure. He did not mention that many of the young players could not achieve his goal. In a 20-game season, every team cannot mathematically win. Some teams win at the expense of others.

Ames (1984) reports that competitive environments tend to elevate the role of ability versus effort in children's thinking about their performance. The motivation of children of all abilities is cyclical.

Children who perform well thrive in competitive environments and are likely to continue participating because they believe achievement depends on factors within their control. Consequently, failure is considered temporary and, therefore, does not reduce self-esteem.

Children who do not perform well, however, believe that achievement depends on factors beyond their control. Failure is viewed more permanently, which in turn leads to lower self-esteem. Boys in particular use social comparisons to determine their standing among peers and corresponding self-esteem (Duda, 1981). Since self-esteem is closely linked to children's social comparisons, the relationship of social structure and other game elements to self-esteem is discussed in chapter 2.

Chapter 2

Game Elements and Self-esteem

Children need key "building blocks" to develop self-esteem in a God-centered way. This chapter addresses the building blocks, followed by an actual account of a child whose self-esteem was shaken for a time. The account will help game leaders consider the relationship between the elements of a game and self-esteem. The chapter concludes by suggesting ways to modify each game element so all children may be included.

Self-esteem Building Blocks

Self-esteem is learned. A child ascribes value to herself by seeing and hearing what others value in themselves, and by experiencing ways others react or treat her directly. Over time, images are gradually shaped and molded and given a sense of value or worth internally. Rainey and Rainey (1986) describe the images as a "composite":

> Like a police department's composite sketch of a criminal suspect, [a child's] self-esteem is a composite drawing acquired from various sources and first hand accounts. Countless sources over time have contributed to his artistic rendering of self (p.37).

Building blocks contributing to self-esteem include worthiness, a sense of belonging, and competence. McDowell (1984) emphasizes that every child needs to build each block adequately to have a stable self-esteem. Stability might be measured by the degree to which people see themselves as God sees them--"no more and no less" (McDowell, 1984, p.31).

Worthiness involves a child's acceptance of herself for who she is. In other words, she has inherent value. Self-acceptance comes from understanding she is created in God's image (Genesis 1:27), given qualities according to His sovereign plan (Psalm 139:14) and personally atoned for by the blood of Christ (1 John 2:2). Leaders can show children they are worthy by following God's example in demonstrating love even when they do something wrong or fail to meet expectations (Romans 5:8).

A second building block to self-esteem involves a child's sense of **belonging**. In general, people gain a sense of belonging by recognizing their interconnectedness to others. God designed people to depend on one another for love (Romans 13:8), acceptance (Romans 15:7) and encouragement (1 Thessalonians 5:11). Interconnectedness in physical activities most often occurs when each person genuinely participates. Genuine participation requires more than group membership. It also requires that a child contribute to the group in a meaningful way. Genuine participation provides security because a child feels accepted by others. A prime example of insecurity stems from being chosen last for a team. Children chosen last may be tolerated by others, but not genuinely accepted. This underscores the importance of determining teams by methods that do not single children out. (See chapter 8 for examples.)

In addition to worthiness and a sense of belonging, children's **competence** or achievement lays a foundation for building self-esteem. Effects of competence on self-esteem are cyclical (Pangrazi, 1982): Successful experiences help children feel competent; competence enhances self-esteem; high self-esteem helps children "take risks" so they may experience continued success. Risk taking in this context refers to a child's emotional willingness to try something new, rather than to physical feats that may be dangerous.

Ideally, a child's self-esteem is not closely linked to competence, since God is primarily concerned with attitude (1 Samuel 16:7) and effort (Colossians 3:23). While this is the ideal to work toward, Christian leaders need to recognize children's inconsistency in applying mature biblical principles. Even if young children are taught that self-esteem comes from God's love and acceptance--regardless of ability, most lack the spiritual and emotional maturity needed to overlook their inabilities, and peer's reactions to them. Therefore, leaders need to monitor children's perceptions of failure so they view mistakes as learning opportunities, instead of as indicators of their personhood.

Children need to understand that mistakes are normal and each person is gifted differently. Failing at tasks can motivate children to try other means of reaching their goal(s).

At the same time leaders facilitate healthy attitudes toward failure, they need to limit the amount of failure children experience. Failing at tasks can be motivating as long as a child's experiences are not characterized by failure overall (Dweck & Elliott, 1984). The same may be said of the Christian walk. Failing to seek counsel (Proverbs 15:22) or to pray (1 Samuel 12:23) does not result in failing the ultimate test (2 Corinthians 13:5-6). So, in the context of a game, a child needs to know that failing to catch a ball or reach a base does not result in failure overall.

"Playing with the Blocks"

Children's play experiences are recognized by teachers, parents and other leaders as a potential vehicle for enhancing character development. This explains, in part, why so many Christian education programs include recreational games as part of the curriculum (i.e. AWANA, Family Camp, Vacation Bible School). Addressing the self-esteem aspect of character development during recreational games is particularly challenging, since the success and failure of young people is more open to scrutiny by peers than in other educational situations. For instance, a child's mistakes on a worksheet are often unnoticed by peers, whereas the child who finishes last in a relay is commonly ridiculed. Seeing recreational games through the eyes of a child may reveal unknown, deeply rooted feelings. Our oldest son's experience as a 5-year-old will be vivid in my mind for years to come. I still picture Brad participating unhappily in games at the neighborhood park--or was he genuinely participating?

Excluding children

Brad entered a game of *Red Rover* on the first day of the summer playground program. At his request I watched from the side, and planned to slip away after activity had begun. Admittedly, I had preconceived reservations about the recreational value of *Red Rover*, since the game only involves a few people at a time. 'But,' I thought, 'at least he'll enjoy being with the other children.' Two teams of 10 formed and stood in lines facing each other. Within Line <u>B</u>, arms were extended sideways with hands joined to prevent a member of Line <u>A</u> from running and breaking through. Then a player from Line <u>B</u> ran to attempt breaking through arms joined in Line <u>A</u> (and so on as the teams alternated turns). I watched child after child run to the other side and try to break through two outstretched joined arms--but not Brad. I watched child after child try to prevent others from running through their joined arms--but not Brad. 'Surely he'll get a turn,' I thought, 'It's just a matter of time'--but eventually time ran out.

My preconceived notions were confirmed. Brad had actually stood there for nearly 20 minutes without having a turn, without talking to anyone. I hurt inside, and I knew he did too. Oh yes, the children did complete crafts and other games after I left. Even so, I wondered if the initial game experience would have a lasting impact. When I returned to pick up Brad, my answer was immediately apparent. His first remark was unsolicited: "I didn't get a turn in *Red Rover*." In other words, he felt excluded. He was somber and did not want to return to the program. My mind flashed back to the initial game, when I watched him fidget in line, with head down, waiting for his name to be called. (Refer to Figure 2.1.)

Red Rover, like many traditional competitive games, tends to exclude players. In other words, some children participate at the expense of others. Brad's self-esteem "checklist" drew a blank. Being excluded meant he didn't **belong**. He was unwanted. Being excluded meant no opportunity to show he was **competent**, even though he was. According to Dobson (1974), lack of opportunity to perform is often interpreted as lack of competence, because perceptions of physical ability can influence self-esteem to a greater extent than actual ability. Since Brad felt unwanted and incompetent, it was natural to feel **unworthy** also.

A week later before returning to the park, Brad asked with concern written all over his face: "Will they play *Red Rover* today"? Reassuring him he would have a good time, I asked one of the recreation leaders to be sure he got a turn in whatever game was played. Unfortunately, a different leader took charge of games, and the same situation occurred again. Brad did not know many other children, and *Red Rover* depended on one group calling a member of the other group by name to "Come on over."

My purpose in describing Brad's experience is not to gain sympathy from others, nor is it to criticize recreation leaders. After all, even when program leaders have the best intentions, all children will not always get a turn during games. However, two important points may be underscored. First, Brad's experience is not an isolated case. During my experiences observing and leading physical activities in the church, camp and school settings, I have witnessed many instances of children being excluded. Second, situations like Brad's can be prevented by providing age appropriate games that include players. Brad's unfortunate experience was as much due to the elements of the game, as

Figure 2.1: Illustration of *Red Rover*

to the game leadership. Even when *Red Rover* is prolonged to give every person a chance, children are predominantly inactive, since each scoring attempt involves a single runner from one line, and two people with hands joined from the other line.

Including Children

The elements of a game need to remain flexible to include all children. Leaders who understand how to modify recreational games to accommodate different developmental levels can favorably influence the self-esteem of children. Entire books have addressed ways to modify games (Morris, 1980; Morris & Stiehl, 1989), although I am not aware of any written from a biblical perspective. The next section of this book provides an overview of general principles for modifying game elements using the "GAMES" acronym. General principles are then applied through particular examples for the game *Red Rover*.

Goals

Goals are best modified by emphasizing the process of playing a game, and by emphasizing products of a game besides winning. Process goals are measured during a game, whereas product goals are measured after a game. While not exhaustive, Table 2.1 highlights suggested goals for the game of *Baseball*. Various goals correspond to different abilities of players.

Players with limited ability should target primarily process goals. Process goals result from breaking down physical and social skills into specific achievable components. A child who seldom hits the ball can focus initially on assuming a good batting stance and swinging at strikes. Later the same child can concentrate on swinging down on the ball and making good contact. If a child focuses on particular components of skills, she may be satisfied with achieving a specific goal, regardless of the products of a game. Furthermore, the child can be fulfilled by giving maximum effort even when specific goals are not reached. Focusing on effort and specific achievements contributes to an unconditional self-esteem, because attention shifts away from the results of a child's performance.

Product goals represent game outcomes, such as the culmination of performing a skill or applying strategy. Players with greater ability may pursue product goals along with process goals. A child who regularly makes contact with the bat could focus on hitting fair balls, and then line drives. Strategy may involve trying to hit a sacrifice fly.

Table 2.1

Suggested Process and Product Goals for Baseball *

Batting

Assuming good stance
Lining up knuckles on bat
Swinging at strikes
Stepping toward pitcher
Swinging down on ball
Actually making contact
Following through with swing
Hitting fair ball
Hitting line drive
Hitting sacrifice fly

Running bases

Running hard on contact
Running through first base
Rounding bases
Running on every force out
Running with two outs
Tagging up on fly ball
Safely reaching base
Stealing base
Scoring run

Fielding ground ball

Assuming proper position
  in field
Assuming proper stance
Charging ball
Getting in front of ball
Keeping glove on ground
Knocking ball down
Fielding ball cleanly

Fielding fly ball

Getting jump on ball
Calling for ball
Getting underneath ball
Holding glove chin high
Keeping elbows down
Watching ball into glove
Using two hands
Actually catching ball

Throwing ball

Holding ball across seams
Stepping toward target
Straightening arm initially
Pointing thumb down
Following through with
  step
Throwing to correct base
Throwing ball accurately
Throwing runner out

Being sportsmanlike

Respecting position
  assignments
Exhibiting self-control
  following error
Accepting umpire's call
Consoling teammate
Complimenting opponent
Shaking opponent's hand

* Italicized items indicate product goals.

Players need to be careful about how much emphasis they place on product goals. Product goals depend on the performance of other players to a greater degree than process goals. A player's success in hitting a line drive depends on where the opposing pitcher throws the ball. A player's success in throwing out an opponent depends on his own teammate's ability to be at the appropriate base and catch the ball.

Alignment

The alignment of a game includes players by giving them equal opportunity to be involved. Equal opportunity requires having equal access to equipment. In some alignments, such as a circle or square, players have equal access as long as leaders prevent assertive players from dominating. Domination occurs when one player intentionally or unintentionally steps in front of others to make plays.

Alignments for some games tend to include players at certain positions more than others. In *Baseball*, players generally consider the outfield (particularly right field) undesirable because few balls are hit that far. In *Soccer*, defensive positions are less desirable than offensive positions because players like to score. In *Football*, less gifted players are often "stuck" in the role of a blocker play after play.

Alignments can be changed to place various positions on equal par with one other. In *Square Soccer* (p.118), for instance, all players simultaneously serve on offense and defense. When a ball comes to an individual she tries to prevent it from crossing her line, then tries to kick it across one of the opponent's two lines (two sides of the square). When field positions cannot be arranged on equal par, players can rotate through positions in an organized manner to allow all individuals to play more varied and desirable roles. Rotating positions does not necessarily mean that all players should play all positions. Every child does not have the ability to play pitcher or quarterback. Placing a child in a position where he walks batters around the bases may do more harm than limiting his participation to less "desirable" roles.

Movements

Children's success performing movements in games depends on their quantity and quality of practice. Quantity of practice refers to how often a skill is repeated. To achieve an optimum number of skill repetitions children need to first practice skills in isolation from games. By working alone or in pairs children are able to increase consistency, without regard to strategy and other team concepts.

Once children achieve basic competency in skills, repetition is enhanced by playing games with small numbers of children and/or by providing enough equipment. This is one reason Werner (1989) recommends that children play net/wall type activities before other games. By contrast, children engaged in a traditional *Kickball* game may only kick the ball twice, and throw the ball once--or not at all (Wilson, 1976). Instead of the common practice of playing one game with 20 to 30 children, leaders are encouraged to organize two games with 10 to 15 children. In addition, leaders might consider having two pitchers and two kickers at a time. The two kickers could run opposite directions around the bases, as in *Double Direction Kickball* (p.119). This format requires more adult guidance--a small price to pay to provide enough repetition of skills.

Quality of practice refers to how well a skill is performed. Skill quality is enhanced by providing a relaxed, nonthreatening practice environment, by giving specific feedback about performance, and/or by breaking skills down into basic forms. A relaxed environment allows children to practice skills at their pace "out of the spotlight." Relays are often threatening to children because so much emphasis is placed on speed and those finishing last are "in the spotlight." Leaders are encouraged to build quality controls into relays, and to end activity after a chosen amount of time lapses, rather than after the last person completes the task(s). Quality control may be achieved by requiring that a skill be performed in a particular observable way. For instance, leaders could require children to dribble a basketball below the waist. This elicits different movement than when players are allowed to dribble the ball at any height out of control.

When all teams remain active until time lapses, it is not obvious which team completes the task the most or least number of times. Rather than comparing exact scores of teams, leaders may ask which teams finished the task(s) at least 5 times (then 7 times; then 10 times). Leaders need to begin with a low enough number that all teams are included in the first inquisition. Since some children have more turns than others on the same team, leaders can rotate which child starts the next relay.

Feedback about performance influences quality of practice by telling performers what to focus on. Leaders are encouraged to balance general supportive comments with specific information about a skill. So, a leader could compliment a child on her overhand throw by saying, "Nice job stepping with the opposite foot," rather than just saying, "Nice throw." Leaders are also encouraged to use specific supportive comments prior to corrective comments. For instance, a leader could say, "I like the way you called for the ball. Next time try to get underneath it a little further."

A third way to enhance quality of practice is by breaking down skills into basic forms. Batting in *T-ball* is broken down because children have difficulty hitting a moving ball. Although more players are successful hitting a stationary ball, higher skilled youngsters may lose interest from not being challenged. This is a drawback of tailoring movements to the lower skilled players only.

In addition to modifying a movement in the same way for all players, leaders may provide movement alternatives from which children may choose. This provides the best challenge for all players, since children of the same chronological age normally span three to four years developmentally. In *Double Direction Kickball* (p.119), for example, players have a choice of kicking a rolling ball from the pitcher, or a stationary ball resting at home plate. The alternative allows less advanced children to perform the easier task of kicking a still object. Since children tend to choose options that provide success, they potentially feel more competent. Over time, the sense of competence contributes to their self-esteem.

Equipment

Choices for game equipment are many and varied. Common characteristics of equipment include the size, shape and amount. Size of equipment needs to correspond to the size of children's hands and/or feet. An overarm throw requires a small enough ball so a child can grip it well. Conversely, catching requires a large enough ball so a child can track it well.

The shape of equipment is also crucial to success. Children have an easier time catching a round playground ball than a football. Yet, when throwing a large object overhand, the football shape provides a better grip than a playground ball.

The amount of equipment in a game dramatically influences a child's level of participation. The more people in a game, the more necessary it is to add equipment. Adding equipment gives opportunities to perform skills to players who would not otherwise have a chance. In some cases, a game may allow each player to have his own balloon or ball, as in *Raindrops* (p. 121) or *Dribble Tag* (p.140), respectively. In other cases, however, equipment needs to be limited, even in large group games. Limiting equipment helps insure safety and facilitates player's social relationships. In a game such as *Frisbee Frame* (p.139), players would spend most of their time dodging frisbees if more than two per team were included.

Social structure

As with enhancing skill practice, leaders can effectively modify the social structure of games by limiting the number of players per game. Organizing two games with 10 to 15 children offers twice the participation as one game with 20 to 30 players. When a game is being taught for the first time, leaders may begin with one large game and form two games after rules are understood. Once children are in smaller groups, leaders can more effectively monitor taking of turns.

In addition to having smaller groups, social structure can be changed by the way in which players relate to one another. In most traditional games, players try to beat each other. Since success depends largely on winning, many children are left with a feeling of failure. Players who focus on the outcome of winning hold this as a condition for accepting themselves. Indeed, Kohn (1992) describes competition as more of a psychological need than a desire: "We compete to overcome fundamental doubts about our capabilities and, finally, to compensate for low self-esteem (p.99)." Even the skillful performer is not insured of high self-esteem according to Walker (1980), since the recognition that victory brings is temporary:

> Winning doesn't satisfy us--we need to do it again, and again. The taste of success seems merely to whet the appetite for more. When we lose, the compulsion to seek future success is overpowering; the need to get [in the game] the following weekend is irresistible. We cannot quit when we are ahead or after we've won, and we certainly cannot quit when we're behind or after we've lost. We are addicted (p.37).

By providing children with experiences in games involving competitive, cooperative and independent social structures, the impact of a particular social structure or game is diminished. In order to apply the principles for modifying game elements, the following section provides three formats for the game *Red Rover*. Game leaders are encouraged to evaluate formats based on the goals they wish to accomplish.

Formats for Modifying *Red Rover*

Game 1

Figure 2.2 illustrates three different formats for modifying the game *Red Rover*. In Game 1, the social structure is modified to limit the number of children to 10, rather than 20 per game. Children probably

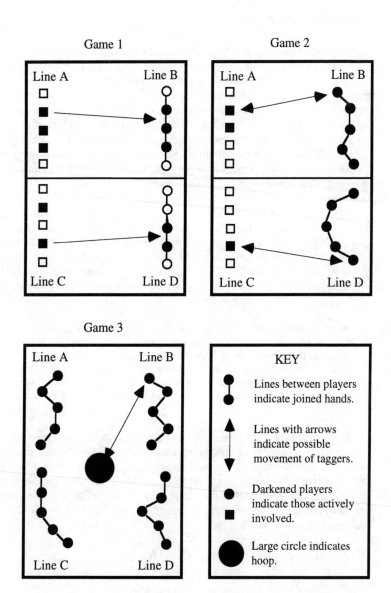

Figure 2.2: Illustration of different formats for modifying the game *Red Rover*.

wouldn't be overlooked on a team of only 5 youngsters. Even so, the game requires additional modifications so that more than 6 players can be active at a time (indicated by darkened players).

Game 2

A second format for modifying *Red Rover* provides for a range of ability levels. Game 2 allows all players to be appropriately challenged by choosing from alternatives provided. Players choose who to tag, and how many times to tag opponents. On signal, Lines B and D dodge about freely (change in movement) within the boundaries without letting hands come apart (change in social structure). Runners from Lines A and C try to tag either end player from Lines B and D, respectively, and return "home" as quickly as possible (change in goal). Home is represented by the child's original place in line. The same taggers repeat this procedure as often as they choose in a minute, scoring one point each time they tag either end player. Naturally, runners from Lines A and C alternate with those from Lines B and D, while players in Lines A and C join hands. Children also take turns as end players of their respective lines (rotating alignment).

For additional challenge, runners could be required to forfeit all points scored for not returning home before the minute lapses. The additional rule would dramatize each runner's choice to risk or not risk multiple tagging attempts. In Game 2, 12 children are actively involved during each scoring attempt, since players are divided into four teams, and two teams move throughout the playing area at a time. Active involvement provides a greater sense of belonging, one of the building blocks to self-esteem.

Game 3

A third format for modifying *Red Rover* involves change for all game elements, and provides more participation than Games 1 or 2. Game 3 provides a common goal for all but the tagger (change in social structure). On signal, all players join hands and dodge about freely (change in movement) in their respective lines. One designated tagger tries to tag as many end players as possible in a minute, returning "home" following each tag (change in goal). Home is represented by a centrally located circle or hoop (change in equipment). Children's performances are enhanced by each other as they all try to move cooperatively in their respective lines with hands joined. As in Game 2, children take turns as end players of their respective lines (rotating alignment). In addition to having a common goal, players in Game 3 are as active as possible, with all players involved during each scoring attempt. (See *Chain Tag*, p.130, for a more extensive explanation.)

These formats for modifying *Red Rover* might suggest that game alternatives should necessarily result in a cooperative social structure. Chapter 3 emphasizes that both cooperative and competitive games can provide worthwhile learning experiences for children in a way that enhances self-esteem. The either-or myth is put to rest, before suggesting ways to monitor people's competitiveness.

Chapter 3

Competition or Cooperation?

Many children's programs involving games are based upon common assumptions regarding the benefits of traditional competition. Each assumption is examined here before giving evidence for the value of cooperative games. Then guidelines are given for monitoring competition so children may successfully participate in recreational experiences with any social structure.

Assumptions About Competition

The first assumption about the benefits of competition might be called **prepatition**--that is, games in which children try to beat each other prepare them to cope with the competitive "daily grind" experienced throughout life. Those who hold to this assumption essentially claim that competition is part of human nature. While the claim has not been substantiated, people may conclude competitive behavior is inevitable, since it is more readily observable than cooperative behavior. Many experts believe competition is learned rather than inevitable, as reflected by Tutko and Bruns (1976):

Johnson and Johnson (1974) point out that in actual practice, "...the vast majority of human interaction, in our society as well as all other societies, is not competitive but cooperative..." (p.218).

A second presumed benefit of competition could be called **production**. Proponents of competition believe that trying to beat others results in the greatest productivity and achievement. Ironically, conclusive evidence demonstrates that cooperation, rather than competition, promotes high achievement and productivity. Johnson and Maruyama et al. (1981) reviewed 122 studies from 1924 to 1980 that compared achievement within competitive, cooperative and independent social structures. Results indicated that in 65 studies cooperation promoted higher achievement than competition, whereas only 8 studies found the reverse effect. Cooperation resulted in higher achievement than an independent social structure in 108 studies, whereas only 6 studies found the opposite. Cooperation was reported as the most advantageous social structure regardless of the subject area or age group.

Participation may be considered a third presumed benefit of competition. It is a widely held belief that children prefer to participate in competitive activities more than in alternative activities. This misconception largely stems from the fact that adults socialize children to compete, and to want to compete (Kohn, 1992). Orlick (1978) found the reverse to be true among third, fourth and fifth graders: "Given the choice, two thirds of the nine and ten year old boys and all of the girls would prefer to play games where neither side loses rather than games where one side wins and the other side loses" (p.177). Children gave many reasons for preferring games with no losers, including: "It's more fun when everyone is working together," "You won't feel so bad cause you lost," and "I usually get a turn" (p.178).

A fourth assumption about competition's benefits concerns **purification**. Proponents have long claimed that participating in sports enhances moral development and the building of character. Moral development is often measured by analyzing people's reasoning about moral issues. Unfortunately, studies have found that moral reasoning is less mature when referenced to a sport specific setting than to a nonsport setting (Bredemeier & Shields, 1984, 1986). The reverse effect would be expected if sports participation enhances moral development. One of the problems in supporting claims that participating in sports builds character, is in defining and measuring

My personal experience indicates that Christians are often among those who assume competitive activities build character. The fact that the Apostle Paul compares the Christian life to a competitive race on several occasions is used as support. With each comparison Paul makes, however, the race metaphor is used primarily to underscore the significance of finishing a course, or persevering through the Christian life (Acts 20:24; 2 Timothy 4:7). The idea of finishing a course could be applied equally well to a competitive game or cooperative game. Interestingly though, other verses directly instruct us to avoid comparing ourselves to others (2 Corinthians 10:12; Galatians 6:4). All children have an opportunity to "win life's race" if they can overcome the world's evil forces (Hebrews 12:1-4). Furthermore, the success of one Christian in the race helps, rather than hinders, the success of another, unlike a traditional competitive game.

Lest I be misunderstood, I am not claiming that competitive sport experiences cannot build character--simply that (a) the evidence is inconclusive for traditional competitive experiences, and (b) God does not expect people to compete against anyone but the devil (Ephesians 6:11-12). At the same time, biblical passages do not rule out competitive games as long as the process of completing the race is emphasized, rather than the resulting victory. Cooperative games and alternative competitive games provide opportunities for children to display character and even to build character. For this reason, all of chapter 4 addresses specific aspects of character development in the context of games.

Some people question whether cooperative activities are as challenging as competitive activities, since challenge within sports is often presumed to be synonymous with beating others. Those holding this view may have limited experience with cooperative activities. Authors on cooperative games offer very challenging activities, some which have been available for three decades. Lentz and Cornelius (1950) suggest *Cooperative Bowling*, which involves knocking down the pins in as many rounds as there are players. Orlick (1982) recommends a *Group Obstacle Course* in which players overcome each obstacle without releasing their joined hands. A more contemporary example is provided by Glover and Midura (1992), who describe *The Rock*, an activity in which all group members help one another simultaneously balance on an automobile tire.

Claiming that either cooperative or competitive games offer more challenge is oversimplified. After all, one can find examples of both types of games with very limited challenge. Instead of claiming superiority with regard to challenge, one could think of cooperative and competitive games as different kinds of challenges. Therefore, by engaging in both types of games (and independent games), players get a greater variety of experiences.

Although similar benefits may be found in games of all social structures to different degrees, benefits of competitive and independent games are often offset by disadvantages. Competitive games tend to produce stress and anxiety more reflective of the American work ethic than of a leisure time pursuit. Stress is one of the reasons cited for why about 75% of youth drop out of organized sports programs (Bavolek, 1993; Orlick, 1978). Granted, competitive games within school or church curricula may be less intense than in organized sports. Yet, enough intensity can exist to counter much of the fun experienced. Although independent games are less stressful than competitive games, social goals are seldom realized since the fun obtained through social contact is more incidental than planned.

Extremists opposing competition believe the problem is competition itself (Kohn, 1992), rather than the social context in which it occurs (Gould, 1984). While I share the concerns of competition opponents, I do not believe we need to choose between cooperation or competition for children eight years and older. Children can cooperate and compete under the proper guidance. Although convincing evidence refutes common assumptions of win-based competition, nonwin-based competition can result in positive ends when quality leadership is present (Coakley, 1990; Martens, 1978). Certainly my experiences teaching and coaching for 15 years support the opinion that competitive games can result in constructive ends when game leaders and participants consciously monitor the way they compete, and the extent of their competitiveness.

Monitoring the Way We Compete

Monitoring the way we compete requires distinguishing between a competitive situation and competitive attitude. Kohn (1992) refers to these constructs as "structural competition" and "intentional competition," respectively (p.3). Monitoring the way we compete requires awareness of our intentional competition in a structurally competitive situation. In other words, once the choice is made to compete with game elements that are determined, how can teachers, coaches and other leaders help players display healthy attitudes and behaviors? I maintain, as does Kohn, that one can have structural competition without intentional competition, and vice versa. In most situations, however, the amount of structural and intentional competition might be most accurately considered on a continuum, rather than claiming competition does or does not exist.

Hypothetical continuums for structural and intentional competition are superimposed in Figure 3.1. The figure could be helpful in monitoring how competitive a particular game experience is. Location of points on the continuum are relative to one another, not absolute. Even though points represent different contexts for the sport of *Baseball*, principles could apply to any physical activity setting.

Professional baseball players operate within a relatively competitive context structurally, given their drafting procedures, multimillion dollar contracts, and quest to reach the World Series. Most players are probably rather high in intentional competition as well (upper right corner in Figure 3.1), although exceptions can be found. When Brian Harper, formerly of the Minnesota Twins, responded to the media regarding his exclusion from the 1993 All-star Game, he saw no reason to have a poor attitude, since God had provided him with a fine family and secure future.

One could place an Instructional Little League experience somewhere near the middle of the continuum. Although the league is structurally competitive, the rules promote less structural competition than found in professional sports. (One would hope so.) Game modifications are adapted to the particular age group, but are inflexible once play begins. The modifications change, to a degree, the way players compete. For example, the league requires that all players participate in at least four innings, including one in the infield, and one in the outfield. All players bat in a regular rotation, regardless whether or not they are assigned a position in the field that inning. Stealing second and third base is permitted provided the pitch has crossed home plate. In addition, no scores or league standings are emphasized.

As with professional athletes, players on a Little League team actually develop different levels of intentional competition, largely based on the influence of the coach and of parents. Our boy's coach, for instance, took several steps to reduce or downplay the level of intentional competition (Point C in Figure 3.1). First of all, he emphasized three goals at the beginning of the season, none of which included winning games:

1. Have fun.
2. Improve skills.
3. Make new friends.

Interestingly, the goals correspond to the top three goals ranked by children who participate in athletics (Gould, 1984). The goals were put in writing to parents, spoken to players at the initial organizational meeting, and reinforced several times throughout the season. The goals are just as appropriate for school, church and other community settings. Additional goals could address aspects of character development at the discretion of leaders.

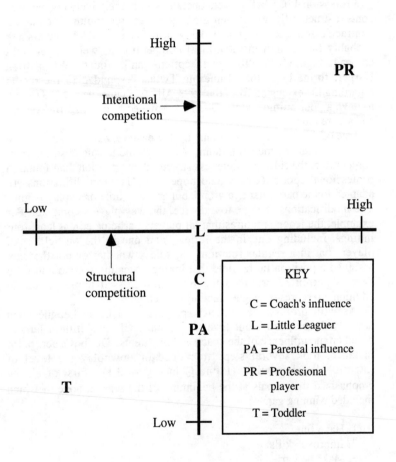

Figure 3.1: Hypothetical relative amounts of structural and intentional competition in *Baseball*.

To help fulfill the goals, the coach rotated all players but the pitcher to positions every inning (more frequently than the league required) and did not emphasize the score during or after the game. Rotating players helped children work on the broadest range of skills, even though fewer runs would have scored against the team with stronger players in key positions. Although some players knew the score without the coach's help, not talking about it still made a statement, particularly since the coach willingly bypassed opportunities to score runs. He preferred to hold a runner at third base for the next batter to hit in, rather than having the runner take advantage of sloppy fielding by the other team.

Weissinger (1994) claims a teacher or coach cannot "have his cake and eat it too," meaning a leader cannot promote competitive games, yet minimize scoring. Since children in physical education regard scoring as the main criteria for succeeding in a game, Weissinger believes leaders need to either (a) accept the importance of scoring to children and, thereby increase scoring opportunities, or (b) reject the importance of scoring and try to change children's emphasis on it. The reason the choices are dichotomous is that our society associates scoring too closely with winning. In fact, winning the contest is often so central to success that many athletes and spectators have difficulty accepting a close loss. If their team cannot win, some people would rather "lose big" than face the disappointment of almost winning. Such a view disregards other viable reasons for scoring. Weissinger (1994) found that children's reasons for scoring in physical education were more tied to personal accomplishment, than to beating the opponent, as conveyed by the following specific statements: "I made a home run in *Kickball*," "I made the most goals in *Hockey*," and "I got the flag back when we were playing *Capture the Flag* " (p.432).

Leaders have at least one more choice in addition to those offered by Weissinger. Like our boy's Little League coach, leaders can accept children's need to score, yet reject the importance of scoring for the sake of winning. Scoring is an important culminating activity. When children play hard individually and collectively, scoring provides a sense of accomplishment. In contrast, I recently watched a youth basketball game in which one team trailed 20-0 at half-time. I would not want my child to be in that scoreless situation--not because scoring helps a team win, but because scoring is a way to measure the success of performing skills and working together. This isn't to say that performing skills and working together cannot be appreciated unless scoring occurs. After all, many alternative goals to scoring were suggested in chapter 2 (see Table 2.1). However, much of the motivation for playing games is found in the various challenges provided. Getting a base hit is one challenge; sacrifice bunting a player to second base is a different challenge; actually driving the runner home presents yet another challenge. With or without winning, the challenge of scoring provides a different sense of accomplishment than the other challenges.

When possible, redefining what constitutes a score helps more children feel accomplished. In Little League baseball, means of scoring is predetermined. In less structured physical activity settings, however, leaders have an opportunity to modify scoring. For instance, children playing *Double Direction Kickball* (p.119) score one point for each base reached.

Parents, as well as coaches, may influence children's level of intentional competition. Parental influence may be largely determined by the degree to which the coach's goals are reinforced, and by additional goals parents have (Point PA in Figure 3.1). In our case, we reinforced the coach's goals before, during, and after each game in some way. Occasionally, when our team was batting, I would walk over by the bench and say, "Who's having fun"? just to make sure that goal did not get lost in the intensity of the game. When another parent could be heard saying, "Hit a home run," I would be yelling, "Just good contact, now" to encourage the player to focus on an immediate aspect of the skill, rather than the outcome.

Additional goals we emphasized as parents were to appreciate opponents and to respect the umpire. I modeled appreciation for opponents by complimenting them for extraordinary effort or performance. When several players from our team criticized the umpire following a game, I suggested that the coach stress the following principles at the next practice:

1. Umpires are human and will make mistakes like anyone else.
2. We need to respect umpire's calls even when we disagree.
3. Calls of the umpire seldom determine the outcome of a game.
   Generally mistaken calls even out for both teams.

Our boy definitely "bought in" to the Little League goals. About one week into the season, without prompting, he prayed that God would help him achieve the goals--spoken word for word as the coach said them. At season's end he prayed again, thanking God that he actually achieved the goals. His positive attitude throughout the season (albeit not every minute) was particularly encouraging, given that his team finished with a "losing" record. Whether or not leaders support the Little League program or the specific coaching techniques described here, the broader principle to underscore is that players were successful in focusing on the process of playing the game, and on products of the game besides winning.

Monitoring the Extent of Our Competitiveness

If the way people compete refers to attitudes and conduct in a setting that calls for competition structurally, then the extent of a person's competitiveness refers to (a) her level of intentional competition when structural competition is low, and (b) when she chooses to enter a structurally competitive setting.

The extent of our toddler's competitiveness is largely determined by our decisions as parents. Trent's experience batting in the back yard is depicted in Figure 3.1 at the opposite end of the continuum from the professional athlete (bottom left corner). Structurally, he has no opponent because his goal is simply to make contact. Granted, Trent is more satisfied when he hits the ball forward than backward. In addition, he sometimes drops the bat and runs in a circle following a "hit," but he clearly is not trying to beat anybody. As long as I maintain a relaxed posture without undue expectations of him, Trent's experience is basically noncompetitive. If, however, I compare his performance with his older brother's performance, the extent of my competitiveness increases and Trent's experience would shift to the right in the figure.

The extent of one's competitiveness is also determined by when the person chooses to compete in a structurally competitive setting. When a person competes is reflected by the age of onset and the frequency of participating thereafter. Parents again contribute to a child's competitiveness (or lack thereof) through decisions made on the child's behalf. Parents who enter a child into organized sports at the earliest possible age increase the extent of a child's competitiveness. Leaders in some school and community sport programs have discretion to help parents make wise choices by delaying the onset of competitive games. Many college students whom I have instructed have told me their dislike for physical activity began in the primary grades as a result of failure in competitive games. Baumgarten (1988) addressed this concern with his plea to avoid regular competition in school settings until age ten:

> There is absolutely no need to spread the evils of competition among our five [to] nine-year-olds in school settings through a steady diet of *Dodgeball, Kickball, Relay Races,* and other mass games, which, by their very nature, prevent so many children from feeling good about themselves and their movement abilities, and which are usually detrimental to the development and improvement of motor skills (p.38).

Leaders and parents, of course, recognize that children of the same age may differ considerably in developmental level. Therefore, no "magic age" for beginning competition exists. At the same time, not many children possess the physical skills or emotional maturity to compete at ages five or six. Consequently, our oldest son skipped *T-ball* and began Little League *Baseball* at age eight after he expressed interest.

After competition is eventually introduced to children, the extent of their competitiveness can be monitored by controlling how often competitive games are played. A first grader may benefit most by experiencing only cooperative and independent games. A third grader might participate in predominantly cooperative and independent games, along with an occasional competitive game. A fifth grader might participate in a balance of cooperative, competitive and independent games.

The exact balance between games of different social structures is not the issue. The critical things to monitor are the values being promoted in recreational games--whatever the social structure--and to what degree players internalize those values. The games and discussions outlined in Part II promote Christian values and character development. By internalizing Christian values, players can keep their competitiveness in perspective. Providing games in which all players genuinely participate and feel good about their experience is a good place to start.

Part II Choices in Process

Part II provides leaders with many games for success to use in a variety of educational settings. The number of games is intentionally limited to 75 to emphasize variety and uniqueness of games, rather than sheer numbers.

Leaders in a variety of settings may utilize games as an integral part of their larger purposes. Character development may serve as the focal point of a game or may be emphasized in conjunction with other goals. Chapter 4 addresses universal aspects of character. Values are generalized to many games and also referenced to specific games with biblical content.

Games in Part II are outlined using a "3-D" format. A **description** of each game provides information for elements discussed in chapter 1. **Directions** for each game provide leaders with a suggested sequence for explaining rules, and possible alternatives. Where helpful, game outlines also include a **diagram** which clarifies boundaries and player positioning.

In classifying games, authors have accounted for the skills involved (i.e. sending an object away [Mauldon & Redfern, 1981]), the object of a game (i.e. scoring runs [Thorpe & Bunker, 1986]), and the type of cooperation required (i.e. collective scoring [Orlick, 1978]). Games in chapters 5 through 7 are organized by the number of players involved, because the variety of games represented does not "fit" well into other classification schemes. In addition, the size of a given group is often a leader's most determining factor in selecting a game. Of course, a large group may be divided into smaller groups of any size to accommodate a game. Chapter 5 contains game ideas for two participants. A collection of small group games is provided in chapter 6. Large group games are the focus of chapter 7. Games within each chapter are sequenced by the recommended ages of participants. An index (p.167) lists games by chapter in alphabetical order. Games from other countries are indicated by an asterisk in the index.

Chapter 8 deals with administering games. Once a leader chooses an appropriate game, the leader needs to provide an environment conducive to realizing the game's goals. Chapter 8 addresses topics such as determining teams, refereeing games, and monitoring time.

Throughout Part II, a balance of competitive and cooperative games is achieved, along with a few examples of independent games. Leaders are reminded that game elements must remain flexible. The choices are always "in process." A particular game may work with one group and need to be modified with another. With a third group, the game may not work altogether. Leaders need to carefully observe players and monitor to what degree all are genuinely participating. More than that, leaders can monitor to what degree all players learn something and feel good about their effort in meeting a challenge, for this is the true measure of a game's success.

Chapter 4

Values and Recreational Games

A characteristic describes what something is like. A person's character describes what the person is like--her very nature. People pursue character development in different ways. Regardless of a person's orientation, however, certain aspects of character are universal, such as honesty, fairness and respect. Even though aspects of character addressed in this book are universal, a person's effectiveness in actually developing character depends on how she goes about it and with what motives in mind. For this reason, aspects of character are best addressed in the context of the Bible. The same God who created us provides the best direction on how to live. Christians are called to live like Christ.

According to the Bible, though, a person's character is tainted by nature (Romans 3:23; 7:18). Sin keeps a person from exhibiting the character God desires. Character may be transformed, however, by trusting in Christ's death as payment for our sins (Romans 4:25; 2 Corinthians 5:21), and by appropriating divine power to avoid habitual sinning (1 John 3:9). Character, then, is an outgrowth of a person's heart condition and thought patterns. This is why Jesus said the greatest command is to love the Lord God with all our hearts...and minds (Matthew 22:37). Because of our vulnerability to sin, we're also told to guard our hearts (Proverbs 4:23) and minds (Philippians 4:8). Why is this so crucial? Because people tend to act in accordance with their beliefs or values.

A leader's role in character development is to influence children's values and help them apply values to everyday experiences. Then with perseverance, character can become more like that of Christ (Romans 5:3-4; James 1:3-4). My experiences as a teacher and parent convince me that values are more easily "caught" than "taught." At some point a child must decide if a value will be adopted and integrated into his life. This is certainly true within the Christian community. A value cannot be forced on a child, just as God does not force anyone to repent and turn to Him. Salvation involves the exercising of a person's free will (Romans 10:9-10).

Leaders of children have an opportunity--indeed, a responsibility--to provide or capitalize on situations involving values. In fact, values are conveyed by leaders whether by intent or by default. If children call each other names, a leader needs to discuss the effect of name-calling on people's feelings. If the leader lets name-calling slide, then children assume the behavior is acceptable and are less likely to stop. Therefore, the Christian response is to intentionally, rather than accidentally, address values. So, reference here to teaching values assumes that leaders may (a) convey information about values, (b) model values, (c) discuss values, and (d) provide opportunities for children to apply values.

Recreational games provide one ongoing context for teaching values. Most children enjoy physical activity, and may be more attentive to values while playing than when sitting in a classroom. In addition, leaders need to address positive values within games in order to counter the barrage of negative role models children see--role models in youth sports, high school athletics, and professional sports. Imagine the impact of a professional basketball player announcing publicly that the owner either replace the coach, or he'll break his contract and leave the team.

Suggesting particular games for teaching values may give the impression that the teaching of values is limited to those games only. Some people get a similar impression when a church highlights missions during a particular time of the year. The concern is that people may misunderstand the intent of bringing into acute focus ideas that should be emphasized on an ongoing basis. This is the purpose of chapter 4--to help leaders integrate aspects of character as a general part of most any game, yet incorporate aspects of character into particular games involving biblical content.

So then, biblical values may be promoted through recreational games in two basic ways. One way is by beginning with an aspect of character, then extending it to a variety of games over time. Honesty and fairness are commonly addressed in recreational games. Issues of respect are less commonly emphasized.

The second way to teach biblical values is by beginning with a biblically-based game. Leaders may teach a game that incorporates particular facts, or historical information about events that actually occurred during Old or New Testament times. Normally, the teaching of facts is followed by a brief discussion of underlying principles and ways to apply principles to character development. Of course, if a problem concerning character occurs during a game, it is best addressed at that moment. What better way to show children that character development is more important than the game itself.

Game leaders are generally familiar with universal values associated with character development. Leaders may be less familiar, however, with ways to relate games to the values they hold, particularly in the context of specific biblical content. This chapter provides leaders with ways to incorporate selected values into games. Leaders who are so inclined may reference their discussion to the Bible verses included.

Generalizing Values to Many Games

This section provides ways to discuss aspects of character with children. Specific dialogue is provided for each aspect or attribute. Discussion could occur prior to a game in which children are expected to display a particular attribute, and/or following a game in which children had difficulty displaying an attribute. Suggested dialogue is given for elementary and middle school age children separately. Italicized portions indicate questions to ask children. Leaders may find the outlines for dialogue most effective when used as a general guide, rather than a stringent "script." Approaching conversations with flexibility enables leaders to adjust dialogue to responses of children.

Diligence

Diligence could be a topic for emphasis in any game. Children may think of exercise as a form of stewardship. People have a responsibility to use all God's gifts as best they can, including the body.

Elementary school age

People try hard in a game for many reasons. *Who can tell me one reason?...What's another reason?...Does God care how you perform in a game?*...He does care how hard you try, but not whether you win or lose. There's nothing wrong with trying to win. But if winning is the main goal, then you're expecting something God does not expect.

Key verse: Whatever you do, work at it with all your heart, as working for the Lord, not for men...(Colossians 3:23). Paraphrase: God says to do your best and to do it for Him.

Working at something with all your heart means working hard or doing your best. Another word for working hard is diligence. If you do your best in a game, that same habit can help you do your best with homework or chores. Let's pray about that:

> Lord, we thank you for challenging us to do our best, whether it's doing chores or playing a game. Please help us develop a habit of being diligent. We may win or lose when we try our best, but you love us the same either way. In Jesus name, Amen.

Middle school age

*Who tried to do your best in the game you just played?...Why?...What are some other reasons?...*One reason people sometimes forget is that God wants you to do your best--to be diligent.

> Key verses: Whatever you do, work at it with all your heart, as working for the Lord, not for men, since you know that you will receive an inheritance from the Lord as a reward. It is the Lord Christ you are serving (Colossians 3:23-24).

*Why would God care about a game?...*Maybe it's because being diligent in a game helps you to be diligent other places, just like being honest in a game helps you to be honest other places. If a person's main goal is winning, then that person probably won't try his best when he gets way behind or way ahead, because he thinks the winner is already decided. So, a person's main goal can be to do his best.

*If you do your best will the Lord always reward you in a game?...*The Lord may or may not choose to reward you right then and there. But if you keep on being diligent, it will pay off eventually. Let's ask God to help us be diligent:

> Lord, Please help us to be diligent. Sometimes that's hard. It's especially hard to do our best at things we don't always enjoy. We don't always enjoy being way behind in a game, but help us remember that whatever we do, we do for you. So help us try our best. In Jesus name, Amen.

Faithfulness

Biblical faithfulness refers primarily to God's commitment to His people (Psalm 117:2; 1 Corinthians 10:13) and His people's commitment to Him (1 Samuel 26:23; Proverbs 3:3). One of the ways people demonstrate faithfulness to God is to be faithful or loyal to each other (3 John 5). The success of some games depends on faithfulness or loyalty among players. Loyalty is especially important to discuss in activities where players have particular roles, or in games where composition of groups changes. In games with designated roles, groups play well when each person carries out his task(s). For instance, in *Pin Soccer* (p.133) players take turns as goalies, halfbacks and forwards. If a player switches to a new position on her own initiative, the team suffers because the old position is left vacant. In games where group composition changes, some players are tempted to intentionally change groups to be with a friend. Players need to be sensitized to ways a game "breaks down" when individual desires supersede group goals.

Elementary school age

*What does it mean to be faithful or loyal?...How can you be loyal in a game?...*In this next game some of you will be changing around to different teams. The best way to be loyal is to play your best for which ever team you are on. Being loyal or faithful to each other helps you be faithful to God.

Key verse: Dear friend, you are faithful in what you are doing for the brothers...(3 John 5a). Paraphrase: Be faithful to others.

Let's pray for God's help in being faithful when we are tempted to be unfaithful:

Lord, thank you for your faithfulness to us. Help us be faithful to you and to others. We pray we will practice being faithful by playing our best for whatever team we are on. In Jesus name, Amen.

Middle school age

*How does God show He is faithful?...How can you show God you are faithful or loyal?...How can you show others you are loyal in a game?...*In the next game each of you will play different positions. You can show you are loyal by playing the position you are assigned. Your team will be counting on you to do your part in the game, because no one else can do it for you.

*Are you unfaithful when you make a mistake?...Why?...*Mistakes do not make a person unfaithful. A person is unfaithful when he doesn't try to do his part for the team.

Key verse: Dear friend, you are faithful in what you are doing for the brothers, even though they are strangers to you (3 John 5).

Let's ask God to help us be faithful to each other in the game:

Lord, you show you are faithful to us over and over again. Help us be faithful to you and to each other. We pray we will practice being faithful in the game by playing our assigned positions. In Jesus name, Amen.

Honesty

Children have frequent opportunities to display honesty during games. Common examples include determining who has been tagged, reporting one's own fouls against others, and monitoring the score. Leaders are encouraged to let children monitor and report their scores when possible, rather than stepping in as "judge." Children are more likely to display honesty in important nongame situations if they develop a habit in relatively unimportant game situations.

Elementary school age

People play games to practice skills or just to have fun. Games can also help people learn to get along. *Why do you need to get along in a game?...*If you don't get along, the game doesn't work very well.

One way to get along is by telling the truth. *Do you ever need to tell the truth during a game?...What about the game you just played?...If someone does not tell the truth, how does that make you feel?...*So, it's important to you that your friends tell the truth during a game. It's also important to God.

Key verse: The Lord detests lying lips, but he delights in men [or children] who are truthful (Proverbs 12:22). Paraphrase: The Lord hates lying, but he really likes the truth.

Let's ask God to help us tell the truth during games:

Lord, we thank you for games and the fun we can have. Help each of us realize that games are more fun when everyone plays honestly. Please help keep us from lying or cheating when we play. In Jesus name, Amen.

Middle school age

*Why do people play games?...What can people learn in a game besides skills and strategy?...*Games can also help you learn more about God and how He wants you to act. *Why would He care how you act in a game?...What are some examples of acting the wrong way?...*

Right now I want you to think about honesty. This is one way God wants you to act. *What parts of the game you just played required you to be honest?...Was it hard to be honest?...Why?...If someone is dishonest, how does that change the game?...*God has a lot to say about dishonesty. The Bible uses the word deceit.

Key verses: Like a madman shooting firebrands or deadly arrows is a man who deceives his neighbor and says, "I was only joking"! (Proverbs 26:18-19).

Dishonesty is not something to joke about, or it may become a habit. Ask yourself if you were honest in this game. In a moment we'll have a brief time of silence. If you did not report the right score, or if you pretended you weren't out of bounds (or another act of dishonesty in the particular game played), you'll have a chance to confess it to the Lord. It doesn't mean you're a terrible person. It doesn't mean the Lord dislikes you. This just gives you a chance to say "OOPS, I blew it. Please forgive me. Help me to be honest the next time."

Let's pray about tell the truth during games:

Lord, we thank you for games and the fun we can have. We also know you teach us about life during games--like what happens when we lie. Help each person here realize there is great joy in telling the truth, even if his or her team scores fewer points than other teams. In Jesus name, Amen.

Humility

Discussion of humility would most appropriately follow a game in which an individual or group performed unusually well. Examples include performing a particular feat, scoring many points, or making a good comeback.

Elementary school age

Your group did quite well today. *How do you feel when you do really well?...Is it okay to be glad?...Is it okay to cheer?...*Cheering is fine as long as we cheer for the right reasons. *What's an example of cheering for the wrong reasons?...*

Some people cheer because they want to make another group feel bad. Or, sometimes people cheer to show others they did something good. *What do we call that?...*God doesn't like bragging or boasting. God wants you to be humble--to do your best and give Him the credit.

> Key verses: But let him who boasts boast in the Lord. For it is not the one who commends himself who is approved, but the one whom the Lord commends (2 Corinthians 10:17-18). Paraphrase: When you do something well, give God a "pat on the back" instead of yourself. He'll give you a "pat on the back" for being humble.

Let's thank God for our abilities, and pray we can give Him the credit when we play well:

> Lord, thank you for giving us our abilities. We know you gave a little bit different abilities to each person. Help us use our abilities well in games without boasting. In Jesus name, Amen.

Middle school age

Your group did quite well today. *How do you feel when you score a lot of points?...How do you show you're glad?...What are some wrong ways to show you're glad?...What do professional athletes do sometimes when they make a basket or touchdown?...*

*What are other words for bragging or boasting?...*One word you may not have thought of is pride. God doesn't like pride. Instead He wants you to be humble--to realize you only score or make a great play due to God's help. *How could you show you're humble after you make a good play?...*

> Key verses:...clothe yourselves with humility toward one another, because "God opposes the proud but gives grace to the humble." Humble yourselves, therefore, under God's mighty hand, that He may lift you up in due time (1 Peter 5:5b-6).

Let's ask God to help us be humble during games:

Lord, thank you for giving each of us abilities. Help us to be humble when we use our abilities well in games. Help us remember to thank you, instead of calling attention to ourselves. In Jesus name, Amen.

Perseverance

Perseverance is a good topic for discussion following a game with a lot of running or other movements that fatigue children. Under these circumstances children can most appreciate the dedication perseverance requires. Leaders might also discuss perseverance as an extension of diligence.

Elementary school age

Someone once said that life is a marathon, not a sprint. That's the difference between diligence and perseverance. Perseverance means to do your best day after day. *What slows people down and keeps them from doing their best?*...God says sin slows people down.

> Key verse:...let us throw off everything that hinders and the sin that so easily entangles, and let us run with perseverance the race marked out for us (Hebrews 12:1). Paraphrase: Overcome sin so you can finish the race God has planned.

How do you know which way to run?...God has the race already marked out for you. So check the Bible to know which way to turn. God may put some obstacles in your way, but he gives you what you need to get around them. *What were some "obstacles" in the game you just played?*...Let's ask God to help us overcome obstacles:

> Lord, sometimes obstacles are fun and sometimes they aren't. Sometimes obstacles have to do with a game, and sometimes they have to do with homework. But either way, we can learn from them and become more like Jesus. Give us the desire and perseverance we need to get past obstacles. In Jesus name, Amen.

Middle school age

What is the difference between diligence and perseverance?...Time is the main difference. People can be diligent in one simple task by giving it their best effort. You are diligent when you remember to make your bed, and make it neatly without wrinkles. In order to persevere, you need to make the bed day after day.

*How do you persevere in a game?...What about the game you just played?...*You can't try to tag someone just once or twice. You need to keep on tagging people until your turn is over. *What does God do when you persevere?...When does God bless you?...*He blessed Job "finally":

> Key verse:...we consider blessed those who have persevered. You have heard of Job's perseverance and have seen what the Lord finally brought about (James 5:11).

Let's pray about persevering when we're tempted to give up:

> Lord, we'll probably never face circumstances like Job. Yet, we sometimes have trouble persevering. We may get tired, we may wonder why we need to do our homework or our chores. Help us persevere in smaller things now so we can persevere in larger things later on. Thank you that you eventually reward us for persevering. In Jesus name, Amen.

Respect

Discussions of respect often center around ways children communicate with one another, both verbally and nonverbally. Children have a tendency to criticize each other's mistakes. Critical words or gestures lead to hurt feelings, especially if game leaders neglect to correct inappropriate responses. Children need to understand that the name-calling and sarcasm so prevalent on television does not set the standard for relating to one another during games.

Elementary school age

Sometimes people make mistakes in a game, don't they? I know I do. *Can someone think of a mistake you made in the game we just played?...Without mentioning anyone's name, can you think of a mistake someone else made?...What do you say to someone when they make a mistake?...What if he's on your team?...*Sometimes I hear some of you calling other people names. That makes me sad, because I know names really do hurt:

> Sticks and stones may cause a bump that soon will pass away,
> While words pierce down into the heart and find a place to stay.

God wants you to treat all people with respect. That means you consider each person important and say things that help, instead of hurt.

Key verse: Show proper respect to everyone...(1 Peter 2:17a).
Paraphrase: Respect every person.

Lets pray and ask God to help us show others respect:

Lord, thank you that you love us the same even when we make
mistakes. Help us show respect to each other at all times by saying
kind things instead of mean things. In Jesus name, Amen.

Middle school age

Sometimes in a game you might want to help someone on your
team know what to do. *What is an example?*...Someone describe an
example from the game you just played...When you give someone a
suggestion it's important to show respect. *How do you show respect to
someone?*...

What are some examples of disrespect?...Sarcasm is a kind of disrespect
people often overlook. It's a way to make fun of someone's mistake
without making it look like you're being mean. It's the kind of humor
in many television shows. *Can someone think of an
example?*...Sarcasm can be all right if you're careful with your words
and tone of voice. God wants you to avoid all kinds of disrespect.

Key verse: Show proper respect to everyone: Love the brotherhood
of believers, fear God, honor the king (1 Peter 2:17).

Let's ask God to help us show respect to others during games or
wherever we are:

Lord, thank you for the excitement of games. Help us show respect
even when we get excited. Help us use words that build people up,
even when they make mistakes. In Jesus name, Amen.

Self-control

Leaders need to discuss self-control in games as it relates to game
administration and game content. Self-control of children is important
for effective game administration in that lack of control results in
wasted time and less understanding of a game once it begins. Self-
control is related to game content in that some games test player's self-
control more than others. Leaders can expect less self-control in games
with higher levels of structural and intentional competition, since
aggression and anger are more prevalent.

Elementary school age

Sometimes people get excited playing games. They're trying hard and they want to do well. *Is it okay to get excited?...How do you feel when something happens that may be unfair?...*Sometimes people get angry. *Did anything make you angry in the game you just played?...*

*What should you do when you get angry?...What's an example of the wrong thing to do?...*God wants you to stay under control even when you're angry.

> Key verse: Be self-controlled and alert. Your enemy the devil prowls around like a roaring lion looking for someone to devour (1 Peter 5:8). Paraphrase: Be ready to use self-control. The devil wants to attack you by making you do the wrong thing.

Let's pray and ask God to help us control our anger during games:

> Lord, thank you for the games we just played. Sometimes it's hard not to get angry at other people. Help us use self-control during games or any other time the devil attacks. In Jesus name, Amen.

Middle school age

Sometimes people get excited playing games. There's a lot to think about and they're trying to do their best. Sometimes people try so hard they get angry when something unexpected happens. *What kinds of things make you angry in a game?...How about in the game you just played?...*

You may be angry at someone else or even at yourself for making a mistake. *What should you do when you get angry?...What's an example of the wrong thing to do?...How can someone lose control without even talking?...*God wants you to listen to other people and stay under control even when you're angry.

> Key verses: My dear brothers, take note of this: Everyone should be quick to listen, slow to speak and slow to become angry, for man's anger does not bring about the righteous life that God desires (James 1:19-20).

Let's ask God to help us use self-control during games:

Lord, thank you for the fun we can have during games, and also for the challenges. One of the challenges is staying under control. Please help us control our temper when we become angry, so we won't do or say the wrong thing. In Jesus name, Amen.

Self-esteem

Discussion of self-esteem could follow a game in which several players experienced difficulty with some skill or concept, or whenever children are ridiculed for their performance. Leaders can encourage players to perform as well as they can, yet remind players that performance does not change a person's value.

Elementary school age

Some of you did quite well with the game today and some of you had difficulty. Other people here might have difficulty with another game. As long as you're doing your best, you can feel good either way. *What are some other ways you're different from your friends?*...Some of you are also better at drawing or spelling than others. God made you unique so you wouldn't be just like anyone else.

How many people here wish you could play as well as a professional athlete?... Sometimes commercials tell us we should "Be like Mike," or be like someone else. It's fine to work hard at a sport like Michael Jordan or Kristi Yamaguchi, but don't be disappointed if God has different plans for you.

Key verses: For you created my inmost being; you knit me together in my mother's womb. I praise you because I am fearfully and wonderfully made; your works are wonderful, I know that full well (Psalm 139:13-14). Paraphrase: I am wonderful because you made me and knew me before I was born.

Let's pray we'll feel good about our performance even when it isn't as good as someone else's:

Lord, thank you that you made each one of us, and that whatever you made is wonderful. Help us feel good about our performance as long as we do our best. In Jesus name, Amen.

Middle school age

How do you feel when you score a lot of points?...*How do you feel when you don't score many points?*...I want to thank you all for trying.

It doesn't matter how many points you scored or if you won or lost. God is interested in your effort. That's why you shouldn't tease others or think too little of yourselves. The spies with Joshua and Caleb thought too little of themselves and couldn't accomplish what God wanted.

> Key verses: ...We can't attack those people; they are stronger than we are...all the people we saw there are of great size...We seemed like grasshoppers in our own eyes, and we looked the same to them (Numbers 13:31-33).

When you do perform well, who should get the credit?...Describe an example of someone you heard give God the credit...(i.e. Cris Carter of the Minnesota Vikings after breaking the single season record for *Football* receptions). Let's thank God for our abilities and ask Him to help us use them well:

> Lord, we thank you for our bodies and what we can do with them. Thank you that you give different abilities to each one of us. We pray you will help us use our abilities well, and feel good about our performance as long as we give 100% effort. In Jesus name, Amen.

Submission

Player's responses to a referee's calls provide a good context for discussing submission. Leaders can teach children the difference between asking a referee for clarification, and arguing about a decision made. The former case helps children play a game more effectively, while the latter case shows disrespect and distracts players from a game.

Elementary school age

Referees (or officials/umpires) help us decide what happened in a game. Sometimes people get angry when they disagree with the referee. *What are some examples seen on television?*...*What are some examples in the game you just played (without mentioning any names)?*...

What usually happens when players continue to yell at the referee?...Even when players are not removed from a game, their minds are thinking about the referee's call instead of the next play. Then they don't play very well.

Key verse: Submit yourselves for the Lord's sake to every authority instituted among men...(1 Peter 2:13a). Paraphrase: Do what leaders say without complaining.

Let's pray that God will help us treat referees properly during games:

Lord, we thank you for referees and know that you place them in charge during games. Help each one of us think about playing well, rather than about particular calls referees make. In Jesus name, Amen.

Middle school age

Sometimes people referee their own games. *Why do people need official referees (or umpires) in some games?*...Describe some examples of professional athletes or fans responding to referees the wrong way...

How do you feel when you're called for a foul you don't think you committed?...How do you sometimes respond to a call you disagree with?...How about in the game you just played?...How can you respond to calls appropriately even when you disagree?...The following principles can help you respond to referees appropriately:

1. Referees are human. They make mistakes like any other person.
2. You need to submit to referee's calls even when you disagree. The game would not progress if several different people made the calls.
3. Mistakes of the referee seldom determine the outcome of a game. Generally, mistaken calls even out for both teams.

Key verses: Everyone must submit himself to the governing authorities...The authorities that exist have been established by God. Consequently, he who rebels against the authority is rebelling against what God has instituted, and those who do so will bring judgment on themselves (Romans 13:1-2).

Let's pray and ask God to help us submit to referees during games:

Lord, we thank you for the games we played and that no one got hurt. We know you want us to listen to referees as we would a parent, knowing you have placed them in control of the game. Help us remember that referees do their best, and that we can only do our best if we think about each play, putting all others behind. In Jesus name, Amen.

Trustworthiness

Discussion of trustworthiness may be linked to honesty, or may refer to player's roles in completing a task involving trust. Honesty leads to trustworthiness in tagging games when players have responsibility to determine whether runners are actually tagged. Leaders are encouraged to let children determine who was tagged, rather than stepping in as "judge." Trustworthiness within specific tasks occurs in many cooperative games where success depends on each person's contribution.

Elementary school age

In order to play this game you have to know who is tagged and who isn't. *How do you know when someone is tagged?...What happens when the tagger thinks someone is it and that person doesn't agree?...*

Here's a simple rule: The tagger will decide. The tagger needs to be honest. If you are honest, others will know you are trustworthy. Runners can show they are trustworthy by admitting when they are tagged, without arguing.

*So, what will a tagger do if a runner doesn't know he was tagged?...What will a runner do if she doesn't agree with the tagger?...*God likes it when you show your friends you are trustworthy.

> Key verse: I put Shelemiah...Zadok...and...Pedaiah in charge of the storerooms...because these men were considered trustworthy...(Nehemiah 13:13). Paraphrase: People who can be trusted are given more responsibility.

Let's ask God to help us to trust people during games:

> Lord, help us treat each other the way we want to be treated in games. We pray you will help us be trustworthy during games by being honest, and by not arguing with people about the way they play. In Jesus name, Amen.

Middle school age

Were there any problems in the game that you want to talk about?...What happens to the game if people argue over whether they were tagged?...Who remembers the rule to use for deciding who is tagged?...

Remember, the tagger always decides. Not only does arguing interrupt the game, but it also creates distrust of each other. *How do you feel if someone doesn't believe you tagged him?...How can runners show they are trustworthy?*...God's word says people earn responsibility by being trustworthy.

> Key verse: I put Shelemiah the priest, Zadok the scribe, and a Levite named Pedaiah in charge of the storerooms...because these men were considered trustworthy (Nehemiah 13:13).

Let's pray and ask God to help us trust others during games:

> Lord, we thank you for games and the fun we can have. We also know you teach us about life during games. Help each of us earn trust by telling the truth, and help us show we are trustworthy by not arguing with others. In Jesus name, Amen.

Values in Particular Games

The remainder of the chapter contains games designed to teach or reinforce values as they relate to specific biblical content--that is, facts and principles drawn from particular passages of Scripture. Physical movement provides children with a fun, concrete way to experience biblical ideas. In addition, children are more likely to remember ideas expressed through actions, than ideas simply seen and/or heard.

(1) ADAM AND EVE

Description

Goals:	Review story of Adam and Eve.
	Use ball skills in game situation.
Alignment:	Standing facing the center of a circle.
Movements:	Collecting, handing.
Equipment:	7- or 8-inch pliable red ball.
Social	Competitive.
structure:	5-8 players per circle, ages 5 to 6.

Directions

Instruct players to hand the ball to a neighbor on either side. Have players continue handing the ball quickly the same direction around the circle, pretending it is a "forbidden apple." Signal for play to stop (with a bell or whistle) and note who has the ball. Assign a letter to the person caught with the ball for "taking a bite." As players "take more bites," have them spell the word Adam or Eve. Emphasize that players do not want to complete the word. Have each player who receives a letter decide which direction to hand the ball the next round. If a child actually spells an entire word, begin the game again or move on to another game. Do not eliminate a child from the game.

Note: Remind children of the foolishness of playing with temptation. The game is not trying to teach players that people deal with temptation by handing it to someone else.

Fact: Eve handed Adam the apple to eat after she disobeyed God, much like handing the ball to someone else (Genesis 3:6).

Application: Obey God when you are tempted.

(2) NAME GAME

Description

Goals: Name biblical information according to categories.
Use striking skills in game situation.

Alignment: Standing facing a partner.

Movements: Balancing, striking one-handed.

Equipment: One 10- to 12-inch balloon for every two people.

Social
   structure: Competitive or cooperative.
                2 players, ages 5 to 10.

Directions

Instruct players to alternate striking the balloon back and forth with some upward trajectory. As each hit is made, tell the respective player to call out the name of a Biblical item from a designated category, without repeating a name. For instance, if the category is books of the New Testament, players could call out "Matthew," "Acts," "James," etc. until no more books can be named.

Select categories based on the players developmental levels. Younger children may enjoy naming animals that Noah took on the ark. Older children could name the fruit of the Spirit or women of the Bible.

In the competitive version, have each player try to be the last one to strike the balloon and name an item. In the cooperative version, have players count the total number of items named, assuming the balloon was struck each time.

Alternative: For additional challenge, require children to play the game while balancing with one foot and leg remaining off the floor.

(3) LET MY PEOPLE GO

Description

Goals: Understand Moses' role in freeing the Israelites.
                     Exercise total body intermittently.
                     Practice dodging.

Alignment: Israelites standing scattered throughout area; Moses'
                     inside hoops; Pharoahs on perimeter.

Movements: Dodging, running, tagging.

Equipment: Floor marking tape, eight pinnies (two different colors),
                     four nerf balls, markers to outline playing area.

Social   Competitive.
   structure: 16-32 players, ages 6 to 10.

Directions

Have one-sixth the number of people play the roles of Moses and
Pharoah, respectively. Give Moses' and Pharoahs different colored
pinnies to wear. Have other players be Israelites. On signal, instruct
Pharoahs to tag as many Israelites as possible with a hand-held nerf
ball. Tagged players become frozen (captive) at the spot tagged,
indicated by dark squares in Diagram 4.1. Encourage Moses' to leave
their safety zones to unfreeze (free) captives by tagging them (depicted
by arrows in diagram). Have any Moses tagged by a Pharoah outside a
safety zone freeze for the remainder of that round. Score the game by
how many Israelites are captive at the end of a two- or three-minute
period. Rotate players to all three roles as time permits.

Fact-1: Pharoah held the Israelites captive (Exodus 1:8-11).
Fact-2: Moses was reluctant to go to Pharoah (Exodus 3:11,13;
4:1,10,13).
Fact-3: Moses repeatedly took risks to try to free the Israelites.
Fact-4: Pharoah refused to let the Israelites go after several appeals from
Moses, and eventually chased them even after letting them go.

Application-1: Persist in whatever task God calls you to do, even when
it is difficult or uncomfortable.
Application-2: God's justice will prevail, regardless how hopeless your
circumstances seem.

Diagram 4.1
Let My People Go

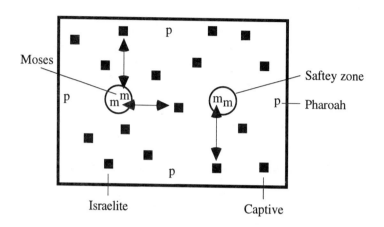

(4) KEEP IN STEP

Description

Goals: Be encouraged to "press on."
Practice throwing, tossing and catching.
Improve hand-eye coordination.

Alignment: Standing facing partner one step away.

Movements: Catching, throwing overhand, tossing underhand.

Equipment: One object for every two people.

Social
    structure: Cooperative.
2 players, ages 6 to 14.

Directions

Instruct players to alternate tossing and catching the object. Each time the object is caught by either partner, have both players take one step back (trying to eventually get as far away as possible). Allow players to take one step in any direction to catch the object, as long as the other foot remains in place. Suggest that players replace an underhand toss with an overhand throw as they get further apart. When the object is dropped, have players take one step forward and continue from that distance.

Principle: The game is a word picture of what our walk with the Lord frequently looks like. We may take three steps closer to the Lord (backward in the game), and then one step in the other direction (forward); then two steps closer to the Lord and again a step the wrong way.

Application: Although our goal is to take all steps the right direction, we shouldn't get down on ourselves when we sin. We are not perfect, but we strive to "press on." We don't take pride in sin, but we look to the future, rather than the past (Philippians 3:12-14).

(5) PASS THE BUCK

Description

Goals: Understand how Adam and Eve responded to being confronted in the Garden.
                 Utilize ball skills in game situation.

Alignment: Standing facing the center of a circle.

Movements: Catching, tossing underhand.

Equipment: 7- or 8-inch pliable red ball.

Social
structure: Competitive or cooperative.
                 5-8 players per circle, ages 7 to 8.

Directions

Instruct one player to toss the ball to a player who is not a neighbor. Have players continue tossing and catching the ball quickly until stopped by the signal (i.e. bell, whistle).

In the competitive version, assign a letter to whoever is caught with the ball. Have players avoid spelling the word "buck." In the cooperative version, have the group see how many tosses they can catch in a specified amount of time.

Fact: Adam and Eve tried to avoid responsibility when God confronted them for eating the apple. They "passed the buck," much like passing the ball to someone else so you don't get caught (Genesis 3:11-13).

Application-1: Obey God when you are tempted.
Application-2: Accept responsibility if you do disobey God.

(6) LOST SHEEP

Description

Goals:	Understand the parable of the lost sheep.
	Exercise total body intermittently.
Alignment:	Standing scattered on two sides of playing area.
Movements:	Dodging, running, tagging.
Equipment:	Markers to outline playing area.
Social structure:	Cooperative within competitive.
	16-30 players, ages 7 to 10.

Directions

Have Team **B** designate a "lost sheep" unknown to Team **A**. Instruct one person from Team **A** to cross the midline and tag as many players as possible from Team **B** within 30 seconds. Although the tagger is credited with tagging a given Team **B** player only once per round, encourage all Team **B** players to continue running until time expires (to provide more exercise and make it difficult for the tagger to remember who he tagged).

Award five points to a team for tagging the lost sheep. Give one point for each additional person tagged. Also award Team **A** a point for each Team **B** player who steps out of bounds (one point per person per round). For the second round, have teams reverse roles. After the first two rounds, send a tagger from each team to the other side at the same time.

Alternative: For additional challenge, require teams to estimate when the 30 second time limit will expire, instead of signaling the time limit with tagging still in progress. Then require a tagger to forfeit all points earned during a round for not returning to the original side on time.

Fact-1: Sinners are compared to lost sheep (Luke 15:7).
Fact-2: God rejoices when a sheep is found (Matthew 18:13).

Principle: Sheep need a shepherd (Psalm 23).

Application-1: Rely on the Shepherd.
Application-2: Do your part to bring people into the flock.

(7) GIVE OR RECEIVE

Description

Goals:

Understand the importance God places on giving.
Exercise total body intermittently.
Improve agility.

Alignment:

Sitting in rows near the corners of a square, facing the center.

Movements:

Collecting, placing, running.

Equipment:

One bicycle tire per group, one center tire with three times more beanbags than the number of groups.

Social
structure:

Competitive.
4-6 players per group, 3-5 groups, ages 7 to 12.

Directions

Instruct Player 1 from each group to run and take a beanbag from the center tire, then run back and place it in her tire. Tell the runner to sit down at the end of her line. (See Team Z in Diagram 4.2.) When the beanbag is resting in the tire, have Player 2 from each group take a beanbag from the center tire and bring it back. When the center tire is depleted, have runners take beanbags from other team's tires, indicated by Team X in the diagram. Tell runners to gradually slide to the right so they may run up the diagonal lines. Repeat turns as necessary until the moment one group has six beanbags placed down in their tire. Since one round takes only a few minutes, play two to three rounds.

After playing the game in the above manner, have players give away beanbags from their tire to opponent's tires (without using the center tire). In this version, begin with three beanbags in each tire, and play until the moment one group has placed their last beanbag down in another tire. The number of beanbags may be changed to make the game longer or shorter.

Principle-1: It is better to give than to receive (Acts 20:35).
Principle-2: Unlike the game, giving to the Lord is not competitive, because we are told to...

Application: ...give cheerfully (2 Corinthians 9:7) as we are able (1 Corinthians 16:2).

Diagram 4.2
Give or Receive

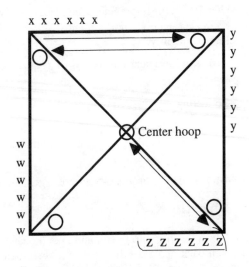

(8) HUMAN TAPE MEASURE

Description

Goals: Understand the sinful nature of humanity.
            Respect and trust others.
            Practice estimating distance.

Alignment: Standing scattered behind designated line.

Movements: Measuring, sitting or lying down.

Equipment: Masking tape, tape measure.

Social   Cooperative.
  structure: 4-8 players, ages 7 to 14.

Directions

From a designated place on the floor, instruct players to estimate how far their group would stretch if they sat down end to end, with legs straight out in front and together. Tell the group that everyone must agree on the estimate. Have players put a tape mark down to represent their predicted distance. After marking the estimated distance, have players actually sit down end to end to determine the length of the group. Then tell players to measure the difference between the predicted distance and the actual distance. Discuss what information players used to make their prediction.

Note: Remove tape marks placed down by one group so they do not "tip off" other groups. If more than one group does the activity simultaneously, begin the groups facing different directions so their predictions do not influence one another.

Fact: All people are sinful and separated from God (Isaiah 53:6; Romans 3:23). No matter how hard people try, salvation cannot be earned. Without Jesus' help, we cannot measure up to God's standard, just as the actual measurement will not be exactly equal to the predicted measurement.

Application: Accept God's gift of salvation, instead of trying to earn salvation through good works (Ephesians 2:8-9).

(9) POTTER AND CLAY

Description

Goals:	Understand word picture of the potter and clay.
	Experience creative expression.
	Communicate with others nonverbally.
Alignment:	Sitting informally in a group.
Movements:	Variety of movements in place determined by the "potter."
Equipment:	None.
Social structure:	Cooperative.
	3-8 players, ages 8 to 14.

Directions

Write down several ideas to be represented by shapes and place them in a basket. Designate one person as the potter and one as the clay. Have the potter select a shape to "mold" (idea from basket) and tell the clay to begin in a sitting or standing position. From that point on, do not allow the potter to speak. Encourage the potter to gradually move body parts of the clay until the desired shape is made. Instruct all other players to guess what the shape is. Have the person who guesses the shape correctly become the next potter, and have players become the clay following their turns as potter. Vary the shapes with the player's developmental ages. Examples include the following:

Animals	Occupations	Household objects	Items from environment
Cat	Firefighter	Bed	Flower
Dog	Lumberjack	Chair	Mountain
Elephant	Policeman	Clock	Sun
Snake	Soldier	Teapot	Tree

Fact: Christians are compared to clay, with God as the potter (Isaiah 64:8; Jeremiah 18:6).

Principle: The more control a person gives to God, the better the pot turns out (Jeremiah 18:1-4; Romans 9:19-21).

Application: Consider some area of your life in which you are taking control. Give control to God instead.

(10) BODY SUPPORT

Description

Goals: Experience a word picture for each person's contribution to the body of Christ.
Respect and trust others.

Alignment: Standing around ball.

Movements: Variety of movements selected by players.

Equipment: 48-inch cage ball or beach ball, two automobile tires.

Social structure: Cooperative.
5-9 players, ages 8 to 14.

Directions

Rest the ball on one of the tires. Place the other tire 30 to 45 feet away. Challenge the group to move the ball from one tire to the other without letting it (a) touch their hands or arms, and (b) touch the floor. Require all group members to contact the ball at all times. Encourage the group to complete the task in several different ways.

Principle: Christians are to bear one another's burdens (Galatians 6:2).

Application: Keeping our burdens to ourselves is like trying to carry the huge ball by ourselves. At some point the weight of the load will overcome us.

Figure 4.1: Illustration of *Body Support*.

(11) DA GA ("The Big Snake")

Description

Goals: Respect and trust others.
                Exercise total body continuously.

Alignment: Standing scattered on basketball or volleyball court,
                depending on number of players.

Movements: Dodging, running, tagging.

Equipment: Markers to outline playing area.

Social   Cooperative and competitive.
  structure: 12-30 players, ages 8 to 14.

Directions

Da Ga originated in Ghana, West Africa. On signal, instruct the tagger to tag other players. As others are tagged, have them join hands to form "the big snake." Once the snake is begun, allow tagging with the outside hands of the snake only. In other words, two hands are available for tagging, regardless of the number of players. If the snake pulls apart, tell all players to reconnect hands before resuming tagging. Have a player who steps outside the boundaries join the snake as if he was tagged.

Alternative: To speed up the game by keeping players more mobile, have the snake divide in half when it reaches six or eight people, and continue dividing with successive snakes. Especially consider dividing snakes with younger players, who have a difficult time keeping longer chains intact.

Fact: Satan is compared to a snake or serpent (Genesis 3:1; 2 Corinthians 11:3).

Principle: Deceit is Satan's primary weapon. He tries to latch onto people with the element of surprise, just as the snake did in the game (Genesis 3:13; Revelation 20:10).

Application: You need to be on the alert in order to avoid Satan. Watch for the areas where you are most vulnerable (1 Peter 5:8).

(12) HUMAN PRETZEL

Description

Goals: Communicate with others.
                Solve a problem.
                Respect other people's spaces.

Alignment: Standing in a circle facing the center.

Movements: Balancing, bending, stretching, twisting.

Equipment: None.

Social   Cooperative.
  structure: 6-11 players, ages 8 to 14.

Directions

Instruct players to join hands with someone who is not their neighbor.
While keeping right hands intact, have players join left hands with
someone else, again not a neighbor. With an odd number of people,
two players will have just one hand tied up in the "pretzel." Challenge
players to untie the pretzel without letting hands go. An odd number of
people will end up in a straight line. An even number of people will
form a circle or two distinct circles.

Principle-1: Each Christian is a member of Christ's body
(1 Corinthians 12:12-20, 27).
Principle-2: All parts of the body are indispensable (1 Corinthians
12:21-26).

Application-1: Just as all body parts are needed to untie the pretzel, all
members of Christ's body are needed to accomplish His purposes.
Application-2: Don't feel any more or less important than other
members of Christ's body.

Note: If more than eleven people are present, give one group the charge
of untying its pretzel without talking. Then emphasize that Christ's
body does not function well if each person tries to "do her own thing,"
just as untying the pretzel is difficult without a joint effort.

Chapter 5

Games for Partners

Games for partners are simple in alignment, since only two people are involved. Although players typically face each other at close range, this alignment becomes more complex when players are required to move back and forth, as in *Butterfly Four Square* (p.75). Many body parts and movements may be incorporated into a game for two, but a limited number are normally used at any given time. This trend is not universal, however, as borne out in the game *Busy Bodies* (p.70) in which players use as many different body parts as possible. As with movements, game equipment may be varied across games for two, but probably limited within a given game.

Regardless which social structure is utilized, players normally interact in simple terms as well. Whether a game is competitive or cooperative, focusing on only one other player is considerably easier than monitoring the play of several others simultaneously. Due to the simple nature of games for partners, many are well suited for primary school age children. For games with a choice of social structure, the competitive version is intended for children near the older end of the recommended range.

(1) BUSY BODIES

Description

Goals:	Improve body awareness. Practice striking.
Alignment:	Partners standing facing each other.
Movements:	Striking.
Equipment:	One 10- to 12-inch balloon for every two people.
Social structure:	Competitive or cooperative. 2 players, ages 5 to 9.

Directions

Instruct players to strike the balloon back and forth, alternating hits. Require each successive hit to be made with a different body part. Encourage players to call out each body part used since some body parts are difficult to distinguish (i.e. finger, hand, wrist).

In the cooperative version, have players count the total number of hits made before the balloon hits the floor. In the competitive version, have players try to be the last one to strike the balloon and name a body part. Do not have players intentionally keep the balloon from the opponent.

Alternative: For additional challenge, require children to play the game while balancing with one foot and leg remaining off the floor.

(2) BALLOON KEEP AWAY

Description

Goals: Improve body awareness.
              Practice guarding and striking.

Alignment: Standing facing partner, scattered throughout playing
              area.

Movements: Guarding, striking one- or two-handed.

Equipment: One 10- to 12-inch balloon for every two people.

Social   Competitive.
   structure: 2 players, ages 5 to 9.

Directions

Instruct Player X to begin striking the balloon in the air and guarding it
from Player Y. Tell Player Y to intercept the balloon and get control
by holding it with two hands. Award Player Y one point for each time
he gets control of the balloon, and a point if Player X lets the balloon
touch the floor or come to rest in his hands. Do not give Player Y a
point if he is the last one to touch the balloon before it hits the floor.

Each time Player Y gets the balloon, have him return it to Player X to
initiate activity again within a 30-second time frame. When 30 seconds
have expired, have players reverse roles for the next 30-second round. A
game consists of six 30-second rounds, with players alternating who
begins with the balloon.

Alternative: To build additional stamina, increase length of rounds to 60
seconds.

(3) HUMAN LETTERS

Description

Goals: Solve problem with partner.
Improve body awareness.

Alignment: Standing facing partner.

Movements: Bending, lying down, sitting, stretching, twisting.

Equipment: None.

Social
structure: Cooperative.
2 players, ages 5 to 10.

Directions

Have players work together to spell each of their first names with "human letters." Beginning with one of their names, instruct the players to combine parts of both bodies to form one letter at a time. Allow players to form letters while standing, sitting or lying down. When the first name has been spelled, tell players to complete the second name one letter at a time.

Alternative: Have players spell more challenging or less challenging words, depending on developmental level. For example, primary level children could spell animal names with three letters, and intermediate level children could spell names of states.

Figure 5.1: Illustration of *Human Letters*.

(4) REACTION BALL

Description

Goals: Practice reacting quickly.
Practice blocking.
Practice kicking accurately.

Alignment: One player standing near goal; other player facing goal, which is 20 feet away.

Movements: Catching, kicking.

Equipment: Nerf soccer ball, markers to designate two goals.

Social
structure: Competitive.
2 players, ages 7 to 12.

Directions

Reaction Ball originated in Luxembourg. Instruct Players X and Y to stand facing the goal, as indicated by the arrows in Diagram 5.1. Have Player Y yell "kick," as a signal for Player X to kick the ball at the goal below the waist. Do not allow balls kicked above the waist to be rekicked. Instruct Player Y to turn around quickly and try to block the ball from entering the goal area. Follow the same procedure two more times from 15 and 10 feet away, respectively. After the three initial kicks, have Player Y kick from 20, 15 and 10 feet, with Player X defending the goal. Award players one point for each goal made.

Diagram 5.1
Reaction Ball

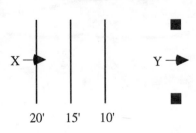

20'   15'   10'

(5) BUTTERFLY FOUR SQUARE

Description

Goals: Improve striking accuracy.
               Incorporate agility into game situation.

Alignment: Standing in Squares I and III (diagonally opposite).

Movements: Sliding, striking one- or two-handed.

Equipment: 8 1/2-inch playground or plastic ball.

Social   Cooperative.
  structure: 2 players, ages 7 to 12.

Directions

Instruct Player X to serve the ball to Square II with a bounce and hit (#1 in Diagram 5.2). Tell Player Y to slide to Square II (dotted line in diagram) and strike the ball diagonally to Square IV. Have Player X move to Square IV and strike the ball to Square III. Have Player Y go back to Square III and strike the ball diagonally to Square I, completing the butterfly pattern. Have players repeat the pattern, counting the number of consecutive hits. Counting starts over when the ball...

1. ...is missed.   3. ...lands out of the proper square.
2. ...lands on a line.   4. ...bounces more than once.

Alternative: Change servers to provide the greatest variety of hits. The server always hits the ball across, and the receiver hits it diagonally.

Diagram 5.2
Butterfly Four Square

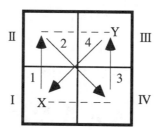

(6) TANDEM TOSS

Description

Goals: Communicate with one another.
                Practice tossing underhand.

Alignment: Partners standing three feet from their respective ends of
                a tire chain that rests on the floor.

Movements: Tossing underhand.

Equipment: Five bicycle tires, 10 beanbags per person.

Social   Cooperative.
  structure: 2 players, ages 7 to 12.

Directions

Have players toss a beanbag into the closest tire, at opposite ends of the
chain, as shown in Diagram 5.3. If a beanbag misses its tire, tell
players to continue tossing until both make it in on the same try.
When both beanbags land and remain in the correct tires, have players
each toss a beanbag to their second tires. Have players continue tossing
beanbags at the same time until one has been tossed into their last tires
(tire #1 for Player Y and tire #5 for Player X). Encourage players to
strategize to prevent beanbags from colliding during later tosses.

Score the game by the number of successful tandem tosses made. The
maximum score is 5, regardless how many beanbags are used. Once
players have scored 5 with the 20 beanbags allotted, they may score the
game by the number of beanbags remaining when they complete the 5
tandem tosses. The best score is 10, since at least 10 beanbags are
required to complete 5 tandem tosses.

Alternative: For additional challenge, require players to begin the game
six feet from their ends of the tire chain.

Diagram 5.3

Tandem Toss

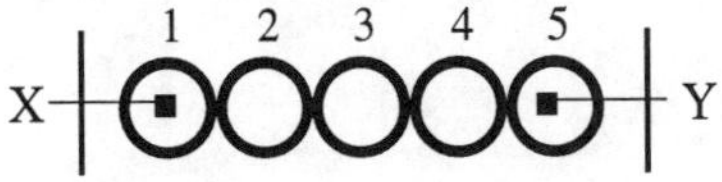

(7) MICA STONE

Description

Goals: Practice rolling accuracy.
                        Utilize hand-eye coordination in game situation.

Alignment: One partner standing by pins and first line, respectively.

Movements: Rolling.

Equipment: Tennis ball, tape, three pins.

Social
   structure: Competitive.
                   2 players, ages 7 to 12.

Directions

Mica Stone originated in Hawaii. Instruct Player $\underline{X}$ to roll the ball from three different lines, trying to make it between the two obstacles, and without touching the obstacles. Score points as indicated in Diagram 5.4. Have Player $\underline{Y}$ roll the ball back and replace pins that move. When Player $\underline{X}$ finishes three turns (one from each line), have players change roles. For the second round, place a third obstacle midway between, and in front of, the original obstacles (indicated by darkened circle in Diagram 5.4). Allow players to roll the ball from any location behind the appropriate line.

Diagram 5.4
Mica Stone

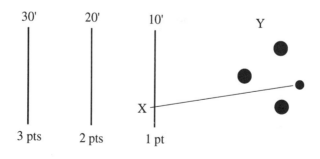

(8) DOUBLE TUG

Description

Goals: Trust one another.
Improve balance.

Alignment: Standing inside hoop facing partner.

Movements: Balancing, grasping, leaning, tugging.

Equipment: Two beanbags, one hoop.

Social
structure: Cooperative.
2 players, ages 8 to 12.

Directions

Double Tug originated in South Africa. Place two beanbags in the center of the hoop. Tell players to grasp same hands and/or wrists (i.e. left/left or right/right) and stand with their feet touching, yet surrounding the beanbags. Tugging on their partner's hand for support, instruct players to lean back in a balanced position. While maintaining their balance, have players lean forward and pick up a beanbag with their free hand. Tell players to place the beanbag on whatever body part they mutually decide on. Require the beanbags to remain balancing on that body part until players grasp their other hands momentarily. When both hands have been grasped, have players release one hand and return the beanbags to the center of the hoop. Have players complete a second round by placing the beanbag on a different body part (and so on for successive rounds).

Alternative: For additional challenge, have players alternate which hands are grasped at the beginning of each round.

Figure 5.2: Illustration of *Double Tug*.

(9) HOOP HUNTING

Description

Goals: Practice throwing accuracy.
                     Practice catching.

Alignment: Opponents standing behind their respective lines, facing
                     each other about 15 feet apart. A hoop is placed on the
                     floor midway between the two lines.

Movements: Catching, throwing overhand.

Equipment: Hoop, playground ball.

Social   Competitive.
  structure: 2 players, ages 8 to 12.

Directions

Hoop Hunting originated in Germany. Instruct Player X to throw the
ball at the hoop, trying to move it toward the opposite endline. Tell
Player X to continue throwing the ball until (a) Player Y catches it on
one bounce, or (b) the ball fails to pass between the markers. Then
have Player Y throw the ball to move the hoop back the other direction
(and so on). Require players to remain behind their lines to throw and
catch the ball, but allow them to move sideways anywhere between the
markers. End play when part of the hoop has been knocked across one
of the endlines.

Alternative: To shorten the game, base scoring on which player has
moved the hoop across the midline when a designated period of time
expires (Player X in Diagram 5.5).

Diagram 5.5

Hoop Hunting

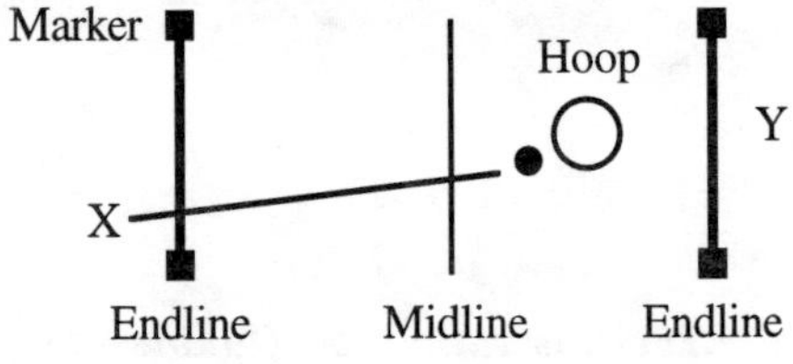

Marker   Hoop

X

Endline   Midline   Endline

(10) KEEPING PACE

Description

Goals: Exercise total body intermittently.
Practice pacing.

Alignment: Standing with partner at chosen starting point.

Movements: Variety of locomotor skills selected by players.

Equipment: Markers to outline playing area, paper, pencil, stopwatch.

Social structure: Cooperative or competitive.
2 players, ages 8 to 14.

Directions

Instruct players to decide on a route for traveling that would take from one to three minutes to complete. Have Player 1 complete the route using a chosen means of traveling, while Player 2 keeps time. Have players switch roles so each person has a baseline time recorded. Allow Player 2 to use a different means of traveling than Player 1. Encourage players to maintain a constant pace, rather than to complete the route quickly.

Competitive version: While alternating roles, have players complete a second and third round trying to get as close as possible to their individual baseline times. Score the game by adding the difference in player's individual times between rounds one and two to the difference in time between rounds two and three. The lower the sum, the better the score.

Cooperative version: Have players add their baseline times for round one. While alternating roles, tell players to complete a second and third round trying to get as close as possible to their joint time for round one. In this version, recommend that Player 2 try to adjust her pace to offset the error in pacing of Player 1.

Alternative: For additional challenge, require players to use a different means of traveling for each round (not necessarily the same as each other).

(11) FIVE BATU

Description

Goals:	Practice tossing and catching.
	Practice reacting quickly.
Alignment:	Standing with partner.
Movements:	Catching, collecting, squatting, tossing underhand.
Equipment:	Five beanbags.
Social structure:	Cooperative or competitive.
	2 players, ages 8 to 14.

Directions

Five Batu originated in Malaysia, where stones are used, instead of beanbags. Give Player $\underline{X}$ the beanbags to drop to the floor or ground. Instruct Player $\underline{Y}$ to pick up one beanbag and toss it in the air. Tell Player $\underline{Y}$ to pick up another beanbag and catch the first beanbag before it hits the floor. Next, have Player $\underline{Y}$ toss both beanbags in the air, pick up a third beanbag, and try to catch the two in the air (and so on). When Player $\underline{Y}$ misses, have the two players change roles. Score the cooperative version by the number of beanbags caught by both players (maximum of eight). Score the competitive version by which player catches the most beanbags (maximum of four).

(12) BACK AND FORCE

Description

Goals:	Practice guarding and striking.
	Utilize different forces in game situation.
Alignment:	Standing facing partner, scattered throughout area.
Movements:	Guarding, running, striking one-handed.
Equipment:	One 10- to 12-inch balloon for every two people.
Social structure:	Competitive.
	2 players, ages 9 to 14.

Directions

Have players alternate striking the balloon. Allow the balloon to be hit horizontally or at some upward trajectory, but not downward. Challenge each player to be the last one to touch the balloon before it lands on the floor. Encourage strategies such as hitting the balloon hard away from the opponent, hitting it softly just before it touches the floor, and/or staying between the balloon and the opponent.

Alternative: For additional challenge, require players to strike the balloon with the nondominant hand only.

(13) BALLOON DESCENT

Description

Goals: Improve body awareness.
Practice guarding and striking.

Alignment: Standing facing partner, scattered throughout playing area.

Movements: Guarding, striking one- or two-handed.

Equipment: One 10- to 12-inch balloon per person, partners with different colors.

Social structure: Competitive.
2 players, ages 9 to 14.

Directions

Instruct each player to begin striking her own balloon in the air, without letting it fall to the ground or coming to rest in her hands. Allow players to strike with either hand or both simultaneously. While keeping her own balloon in the air, challenge a player to make the opponent's balloon land on the floor. This may occur directly by hitting the opponent's balloon at the floor, or indirectly by standing between the opponent and her balloon.

Chapter 6

Games for Small Groups

Games for small groups are generally more complex than games for partners, and less complex than games for large groups. Although many small group games are more suited to upper elementary and middle school players, primary school children can successfully participate, particularly in settings where adults can play with children. Alignments are more varied than with partner games, since just two people cannot stand in a circle or square shape, as in *Beach Ball Bonanza* (p.103) and *Clockwise Four Square* (p.87), respectively. Although movements and equipment utilized in small group games are not necessarily more complex than in partner games, players often need to observe and respond to the play of several other people. This is particularly true, given that anywhere from 3 to 12 players constitutes a small group.

Small group games provide a good atmosphere for fostering social interaction. Input from more than two people is possible, yet players do not become "lost in the shuffle" as they might in large groups. Leaders cannot assume players necessarily cooperate just because they are placed in small groups, however. The input from a given person depends on the size of the small group and the initiative of the person.

In addition to group size and initiative, group members may lack specific cooperative skills needed. In games where group communication and problem solving are stated goals (i.e. *Human Tape Measure*, p.62; *Invent a Course*, p.100), leaders are encouraged to assign responsibilities within groups. Assigning responsibilities allows all participants to take an active role. In *Human Tape Measure*, for instance, one player can record estimates, another can determine the order of play, and still another can record distance. Over a few trials, all participants can assume one of the responsibilities. Additional roles of players are discussed in chapter 8.

(1) CLOCKWISE FOUR SQUARE

Description

Goals: Practice striking.
                     Improve hand-eye coordination.

Alignment: One player standing in each square.

Movements: Striking one- or two-handed.

Equipment: 8 1/2-inch playground or plastic ball.

Social   Cooperative.
  structure: 3-4 players, ages 5 to 8.

Directions

Instruct Player <u>W</u> to serve the ball to Player <u>X</u> with a bounce and a hit (#1 in Diagram 6.1). Tell other players to continue hitting the ball clockwise, letting it bounce after each hit (#2-4 in diagram). Have players keep score by counting the number of consecutive hits until the ball (a) is missed, (b) lands on a line, or (c) lands out of the proper square. If three people play, the ball will travel in the path of a triangle between three squares (depicted on right side of diagram).

Alternatives: For variety, have players reverse the path of the ball to practice receiving it from the other direction. For additional challenge, have players hit the ball with their nondominant hands only and/or hit the ball as many times as possible in a specified time frame.

Diagram 6.1
Clockwise Four Square

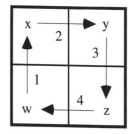 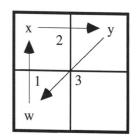

(2) LOOP DA HOOP

Description

Goals:	Communicate with others.
	Solve a problem.
	Utilize flexibility.
Alignment:	Standing in a circle facing the center.
Movements:	Balancing, bending, grasping, stretching.
Equipment:	One or two hoops.
Social structure:	Cooperative or cooperative within competitive.
	5-10 players, ages 5 to 12.

Directions

Instruct players to hold hands in a circle with a hoop hanging between two people. On signal, tell the group to pass the hoop around the circle without letting any hands go. Encourage players to try different strategies to help their neighbors position the hoop. The task is finished when the hoop returns to its initial position. With eight or more players, add a second hoop across from the first hoop. Once a group has completed the task, score the cooperative version by how many hoops a group can pass around the circle in a specified time frame. (Continue passing the same hoop[s] around successive times until time expires.) Score the cooperative within competitive version by comparing the times of two or more groups.

Alternative: For additional challenge, suggest that players try to pass the hoops without letting them touch the floor.

Figure 6.1: Illustration of *Loop da Hoop*.

(3) DODGING THE DISC

Description

Goals:	Use locomotor skills in game situation. Practice dodging.
Alignment:	Standing scattered within half or all of a volleyball court, depending on number of players.
Movements:	Dodging, galloping, running, skipping, sliding, walking.
Equipment:	Drum and beater, frisbee, one hoop for all but one person, markers to outline playing area.
Social structure:	Competitive. 5-10 players, ages 7 to 10.

Directions

Have a drum and beater on hand, and designate a tagger to begin with a frisbee. When you hit the drum, instruct all players except the tagger to travel holding a hoop throughout the playing area. Require hoops to remain vertical and in contact with the floor. Allow players to walk, run, gallop, slide, or skip, since other forms of locomotion would cause their hoops to leave the floor. Have players change means of traveling each time you hit the drum. Tell the tagger to travel in the same way as other players while trying to throw the frisbee through a hoop. When the frisbee passes through a hoop, have the tagger change places with that player to begin another round.

Alternative: For variety, hold the form of locomotion constant for a round, while varying the direction of travel. In this case, have all players change directions each time the drum is hit.

(4) MONKEY ON A ROPE

Description

Goals: Practice passing and catching.
Communicate with others.

Alignment: Standing inside bicycle tire forming a circle around a suspended rope.

Movements: Catching, grasping, passing two-handed, swinging.

Equipment: Two different colored playground balls, one tire per person, rope suspended from ceiling or tree.

Social
structure: Cooperative.
5-7 players, ages 7 to 10.

Directions

Give a ball to two players who are not "neighbors." On signal, tell each player to pass the ball using two hands to someone else in the circle. Options for Player F are indicated by lines in Diagram 6.2. Allow passes to bounce once or travel through the air. Challenge players to continue making as many passes as possible during one minute, individually counting their scores. Award the group one point for each pass caught (sum of individual scores), as long as...

1. ...people passing and receiving the ball keep at least one foot inside their tires.
2. ...passes go to players who are not immediate neighbors.
3. ...passes do not hit the suspended rope (darkened circle in Diagram 6.2).

If one or more of the rules is violated, have the person who passed the ball get the rope and return to his tire. Have that player become a "monkey on a rope" by swinging to someone else's tire (besides an immediate neighbor) and touching his feet down inside that tire. If both balls are involved in a violation, then instruct both players who passed the balls to swing on the rope before passes resume.

Alternative: For additional challenge, have players swing the rope prior to beginning the exchange of balls.

Diagram 6.2
Monkey on a Rope

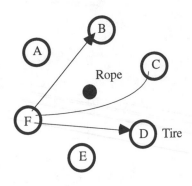

(5) FOUR SQUARE ROTATION

Description

Goals: Exercise total body continuously.
              Practice striking two-handed.

Alignment: Two players standing in diagonally opposite squares;
              one player standing behind each of the other players,
              outside the squares.

Movements: Running, striking two-handed.

Equipment: 8 1/2-inch playground or plastic ball.

Social   Cooperative.
   structure: 4 players, ages 7 to 11.

Directions

Have Player W serve the ball to Player X with a bounce and a two-hand
hit (#1 in Diagram 6.3). Then have Player W run to the right (#2 in
diagram) around the opposite square and line up in Player Z's position.
While Player W is running, tell Player X to hit the ball to Player Y
(#3) and run around the opposite square and line up in Player Y's
original position. Count the number of consecutive hits until the ball
(a) is missed, (b) bounces twice, or (c) lands on a line or out of bounds.

Diagram 6.3
Four Square Rotation

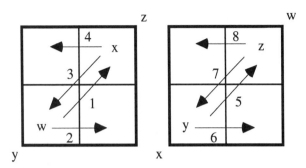

(6) CENTIPEDE

Description

Goals:	Respect and trust others. Improve agility.
Alignment:	Sitting, kneeling, or laying on a scooter behind a line in any formation.
Movements:	Grasping, scooting.
Equipment:	One scooter per person.
Social structure:	Cooperative. 4-12 players, ages 7 to 11.

Directions

Challenge players to advance their scooters to the other side of the playing area (about 30 feet), while remaining linked in some way. If the centipede breaks apart at any moment, have players begin again from behind the initial line. Score the game based on distance or by time. In the former case, award 25 points for having all scooters cross each quarter of the playing area:

> All scooters make it 1/4 of the way = 25 points.
> All scooters make it 1/2 of the way = 50 points.
> All scooters make it 3/4 of the way = 75 points.
> Everyone in group crosses the endline = 100 points.

Score the game based on time after groups make it across the endline. Time successive attempts and see if a given group can beat their own score.

Alternative: Repeat the activity with all group members in a different position on the scooter.

(7) BARREL BALL

Description

Goals:	Communicate with others. Practice striking one-handed. Practice sequencing.
Alignment:	Standing facing one another two steps away from barrel, with a circle on the floor one step away from barrel.
Movements:	Striking one-handed.
Equipment:	8 1/2-inch nerf or plastic ball, one paddle per person, large barrel or garbage can.
Social structure:	Cooperative. 3-6 players, ages 7 to 12.

Directions

Instruct players to strike the ball among themselves in the air using a paddle. Tell players to strike the ball into the barrel with each player hitting the ball before scoring. Allow the same person to strike the ball more than once, but not twice in succession. With younger players, score the game by task completion, or successfully having each person hit the ball before it lands in the barrel. With older players, score the game by the number of rounds required to have each player make the last hit before the ball goes in the barrel (minimum of three rounds for three players). A round consists of a successful sequence in which a new player makes the last hit, or an unsuccessful sequence that results in one of the following:

1. The ball hits the floor.
2. A player crosses the taped circle.
3. The same player hits the ball twice in a row.
4. The ball goes in the barrel before each person hits it.
5. The same player hits the ball last before it goes in the barrel.

Alternative: For additional challenge, move the restraining line further away from the barrel.

(8) LOST IN SPACE

Description

Goals:	Respect and trust others.
	Strengthen arms.
Alignment:	Standing in a circle with each person inside a tire.
Movements:	Grasping, swinging.
Equipment:	One bicycle tire for each person, rope suspended from ceiling or tree in center of tire circle.
Social structure:	Cooperative.
	5-9 players, ages 7 to 12.

Directions

Have each tire represent a planet, and the rope represent oxygen (darkened circle in Diagram 6.4). Designate the person at planet earth as the initial "rescuer." Have the rescuer swing to any other planet trying to carry oxygen to the stranded astronaut. The mission is successful if the rescuer can (a) name a new planet, and (b) touch down inside the new tire without touching the floor outside the tire. Following "unsuccessful" missions, require the astronaut to attempt the rescue again. Allow the astronaut being rescued to help by grabbing the rescuer as she comes.

Have each rescued astronaut change places with the initial rescuer on the rope. Tell the new rescuer to swing to another planet carrying oxygen. Repeat the sequence until all planets have been reached, and the last astronaut returns to earth. Score the game by the number of swings on the rope required to complete the circuit (minimum number of swings is equal to the number of players). Once players achieve the minimum number of swings, suggest that they try to complete the circuit more quickly.

Alternative: For less challenge, have an extra astronaut begin at earth (two people inside that tire). This gives help to the initial rescuer leaving, and to the last astronaut returning to earth.

Diagram 6.4

Lost in Space

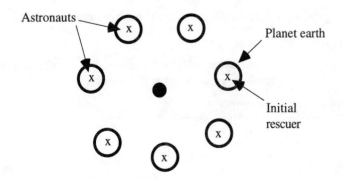

(9) FRUIT OF THE ROOM

Description

Goals: Classify fruit and other selected items.
Practice tossing and catching.

Alignment: Sitting in a circle facing the center.

Movements: "Bopping," catching, passing.

Equipment: 8 1/2-inch playground or plastic ball, two regular adult socks stuffed inside a knee sock (with a knot tied to keep the socks in place).

Social
structure: Competitive.
6-10 players, ages 7 to 12.

Directions

Designate a tagger to sit in the center of the circle holding the knee sock. Give the ball to a player on the circle. Instruct that player to say the name of a fruit and then pass the ball to another player. Tell each player receiving the ball to name another fruit and release the ball, without repeating the same fruit during the same round. Have the tagger try to follow the path of the ball and "bop" someone with the sock below the shoulders before that player can release the ball. Have the tagger change places with a circle player when one of the following situations occurs:

1. The tagger bops a player before he releases the ball.
2. A circle player passes an uncatchable ball.
3. A circle player fails to catch the ball.
4. A circle player repeats the name of a fruit during that round.

To avoid disagreements, have the tagger decide whether an error is due to the pass or catch. Consider a ball that hits the tagger a passing error automatically. Score one point for each time a given player goes to the center. (Players do not want points.)

Alternatives: For variety, provide different items for players to classify (i.e. colors, months, vegetables). For additional challenge, require that no pass be returned directly to the same person who previously had the ball.

(10) HUMAN MACHINERY

Description

Goals: Communicate with others.
                        Improve body awareness.

Alignment: Standing facing other group members.

Movements: Variety of movements selected by the group.

Equipment: None.

Social   Cooperative.
    structure: 4-8 players per group, ages 7 to 12.

Directions

Challenge players to use their bodies to make a "human machine" with
everyone attached in some way. Machines must satisfy a group of
specific characteristics. Examples include, but are not limited to:

1. One body part moving slowly; one part moving quickly.
2. One body part moving at a low level; one part moving at a high
   level.
3. One moving part central to the body (i.e. head, shoulders, trunk,
   hips); one moving part peripheral to the body (i.e. fingers,
   hands, wrist, toes, feet, ankles).

Allow players to fulfill characteristics of machines separately or jointly.
For instance, a person's head may move slowly at a high level. When
one machine is completed, encourage players to satisfy the same
characteristics in different ways. Award points for task completion and
for creativity. Determine creativity points by the name, shape and
sound effects of the machine.

Alternatives: Increase or decrease task difficulty by adding to, or
subtracting from, the number of required characteristics, respectively.
For variety, change the type of required characteristics in the machine
(i.e. one body part moving under another; one body part moving over
another).

Figure 6.2: Illustration of *Human Machinery*.

(11) INVENT A COURSE

Description

Goals: Communicate with others.
                Practice selected motor skills and abilities.

Alignment: Determined by the group.

Movements: Variety of movements selected by the group.

Equipment: Distributed by leader to each group.

Social   Cooperative set-up, independent play.
   structure: 3-6 players per group, ages 7 to 14.

Directions

Determine groups and send each to a designated location where equipment is waiting. Provide different equipment for each group. Instruct groups to incorporate their equipment into an obstacle course with the following parameters:

1. Select at least three safe movements or motor skills to perform.
2. Select movements that involve the whole body.
3. Provide a choice of movements for performers somewhere in the course.

Have each group briefly discuss (a) what movements to use, and (b) how to use equipment. Through trial and error, have groups set up an obstacle course for others to try. If desired, assign specific group roles to participants as suggested in chapter 8. When the courses are ready, tell one member from each group to remain at his "home" course to explain it, while the rest of the groups rotate to the next course. In the second rotation, have a different group member return home to explain the activity to the next group (and so on). Rotate groups to as many courses as time allows.

Note: Although Figure 6.3 includes a ball to indicate variety, courses are best distinguished from *Invent a Game* (p.102) by disallowing object control movements.

Figure 6.3: Illustration of *Invent a Course*.

(12) INVENT A GAME

Description

Goals: Communicate with others.
                 Practice selected movements or motor skills.

Alignment: Determined by the group.

Movements: Variety of movements selected by the group.

Equipment: Distributed by leader to each group.

Social   Cooperative set-up, cooperative or competitive play.
structure: 3-6 players per group, ages 7 to 14.

Directions

Determine groups and send each to a designated location where equipment is waiting. Provide different equipment for each group. Instruct groups to incorporate their equipment into a game with the following parameters:

1. Games are designed for small groups (the number of people in each group).
2. All people need to be active most of the time.
3. Incorporate at least one object control movement.
4. Provide a choice of movements for performers somewhere in the game.

Have each group briefly discuss (a) what movements to use, and (b) how to use equipment. Through trial and error, have groups set up a game for others to play. If desired, assign specific group roles to participants as suggested in chapter 8. When the games are ready, tell one member from each group to remain at her "home" game to explain it, while the rest of the groups rotate to the next game. In the second rotation, have a different group member return home to explain it to the next group (and so on). Rotate groups to as many games as time allows.

Note: Although invented games would not have to include object control movements, requiring at least one object control movement helps distinguish the games from *Invent a Course* (p.100).

(13) BEACH BALL BONANZA

Description

Goals: Practice striking.
                Improve sense of timing.

Alignment: Standing on a circle facing the center with equal
                spacing between players.

Movements: Striking one- or two-handed.

Equipment: One 36- or 48-inch beach ball per group.

Social   Cooperative.
   structure: 6-10 players per circle, ages 7 to 14.

Directions

Challenge players to hit the beach ball as many times as they can
without (a) letting it land on the floor, and (b) the same person hitting
it twice in a row. Allow one foot to step off the circle to reach the
ball, as long as one foot always remains on the circle. Award the group
25 points for hitting the ball as many times as there are people. Give
50 points for hitting the ball twice as many times as there are people in
the group. Continue adding 25 points for each multiple of hits. (Three
times the number of group members equals 75 points.)

Note: If need be, form the circle with individual markers for players to
stand on. Then have players always keep at least one foot on their
markers.

Alternative: For additional challenge, move the group back to a larger
circle and double all scores.

(14) ROPE RESCUE

Description

Goals: Respect and trust others.
                Improve upper arm strength.

Alignment: One player laying on back behind near endline; other
                players standing in a line beyond far endline.

Movements: Grasping, tugging.

Equipment: Tug-of-war rope.

Social   Cooperative.
   structure: 5-10 players, ages 7 to 14.

Directions

Instruct the person lying down ("injured party") to grasp the rope with
two hands. Tell other players to hold the rope at waist level and pull
hand-over-hand to "rescue" their teammate. (Do not have players walk
while holding the rope.) The teammate is rescued when his entire body
crosses the far endline (about 30 feet).

Time how long it takes to complete the rescue. Try the game again
with each person as the injured party. Encourage older players to record
all scores and compute the average.

Note: If pulling teammates across the floor causes too much friction,
have players pull teammates across a large plastic tarp taped to the
floor.

(15) JAM JUMPING

Description

Goals: Respect and trust others.
                 Exercise total body intermittently.
                 Practice entering jump rope.
                 Improve rhythmical ability.

Alignment: Standing next to rope facing the same direction; two
                 players ready to twirl rope.

Movements: Jumping, twirling.

Equipment: One 25- to 30-foot jump rope per group.

Social   Cooperative.
  structure: 5-12 players, ages 8 to 12.

Directions

Challenge jumpers "inside" the rope to "jump in a jam" with as many
teammates as possible. Award points for the number of people
continuously jumping for 5 or 10 seconds, depending on experience of
jumpers. Start counting seconds after all players are jumping:

    3 people = 25 points.
    5 people = 50 points.
    7 people = 75 points.
    9 people =100 points.

Alternatives: For additional challenge, have players enter the rope
through the "front door" and jump for 5 or 10 seconds. Double the
score above for the respective number of people. For still more
challenge, have players enter the rope through the "back door" and jump
for 5 or 10 seconds. Triple the original score above for the respective
number of people.

(16) FLEECE AND FLEE

Description

Goals:	Communicate with others.
	Utilize catching and throwing in game situation.
Alignment:	Sitting on a scooter, scattered throughout playing area.
Movements:	Catching, scooting, tagging, throwing overhand, tossing underhand.
Equipment:	Fleece (yarn) ball, two different colored jerseys, one scooter per person, markers to outline playing area.
Social structure:	Cooperation within competition.
	6-10 players, ages 8 to 12.

Directions

Instruct all players to sit on a scooter, wearing different colored jerseys to designate teams. Have the team with the yarn ball exchange it back and forth among themselves as many times as possible while trying to flee from the other team. Do not allow the defensive team to make physical contact with the fleers except for tagging purposes. Award the fleers one point for each consecutive catch. Have teams change roles (and, therefore, start over counting) when one of the following conditions occurs:

1. The defensive team retrieves a loose ball.
2. The defensive team intercepts the ball.
3. The defensive team tags a fleer who has the ball.
4. One of the fleers leaves the boundaries.
5. One of the fleers throws the ball out of bounds.

Alternative: For additional challenge, require the yarn ball to be thrown to a different player than the person who last had possession.

(17) THE FLY

Description

Goals: Improve hand-eye coordination.
               Practice reacting quickly to ball.

Alignment: Standing in a line abreast, facing the leader, who is 8 to
               10 feet away.

Movements: Catching, passing.

Equipment: One playground ball or volleyball.

Social   Competitive.
structure: 4-6 players, ages 8 to 12.

Directions

The Fly originated in France. Instruct players in the line to clasp their
hands together. Give the leader the ball and tell her to pass it in the air
to someone in the line. Tell that player to catch the ball, return it in
the same manner, and reclasp her hands. Award a line player a "fly," or
point for each catch. Encourage the leader to occasionally fake a pass to
tempt a line player to unclasp hands unnecessarily. When this occurs,
subtract one fly from the player who makes the error. When a player
earns 10 flies, appoint her as the new leader. Adjust the distance
between the leader and group as necessary.

Note: The larger the group, and/or the less time available, the more
need to rotate leaders when a player earns fewer flies.

(18) BLANKET LAUNCH

Description

Goals: Communicate with others.
                    Improve sense of timing.

Alignment: Standing around blanket, equally spaced, facing middle.

Movements: Cushioning, lifting.

Equipment: One blanket and playground ball per group.

Social   Cooperative.
   structure: 4-7 players, ages 8 to 14.

Directions

Instruct players to grasp the edge of a blanket, holding it waist high. With the ball in the center of the blanket, have players "launch" it vertically in the air and catch it. Tell the group to repeat the launch and catch as many times as possible, with each launch going higher than the previous one. (Players begin with a low toss.) Allow the ball to come to a stop between tosses. Require the group to begin again when one of the following conditions occurs:

1. The ball lands on the floor.
2. A player touches the ball.
3. A launch does not go higher than the previous one.

Alternative: For variety, challenge players to repeat the game with each toss going lower than the previous one. (Players begin with a high toss.)

Figure 6.4: Illustration of *Blanket Launch*.

(19) ADVANTAGE

Description

Goals: Practice basketball skills in game situation.
               Exercise total body intermittently.

Alignment: Offensive players standing with the ball at half
               court; one more player on offense than on defense.

Movements: Dribbling, guarding, passing, rebounding, shooting.

Equipment: Child or youth size basketball.

Social   Cooperative within competitive, independent scoring.
  structure: 5 or 7 players, ages 8 to 14.

Directions

Instruct offensive players to use their "advantage" to score a basket. When a basket is made, award each offensive player a point, and have the same players begin with the ball from half court again. Tell defensive players to intercept the ball or get a rebound to prevent a score. When a defensive player gets the ball, have him change places with the offensive player who last touched the ball. Have the new offensive team take the ball back to half court and begin a new turn.

When the ball goes out of bounds, allow the current offensive team to retain possession since no defensive player actually had the ball under control. Restrict the same offensive players to scoring three times consecutively. When this occurs, have the oldest offensive player automatically change places with the youngest defensive player. Have players individually keep track of their running scores.

Note: Substitute a soccer ball or floor hockey equipment for the basketball, in order to practice passing and shooting with feet or sticks, respectively.

(20) JUGGLEMANIA

Description

Goals: Improve hand-eye coordination.
                 Improve sense of timing.
                 Practice concentrating.

Alignment: Standing in a circle facing the center.

Movements: Catching, tossing underhand.

Equipment: One yarn or tennis ball for every two people.

Social   Cooperative.
  structure: 6-11 players, ages 9 to 14.

Directions

Designate a leader to put balls in play (Player 8 in Diagram 6.5). Instruct the leader to toss a ball across the circle to someone else. Tell players to continue tossing the ball until all have caught it, without tossing it to a neighbor, and without tossing it to the same person twice. Numbers in the diagram illustrate one possible sequence. Have players repeat the sequence until they know it well. Then have the leader toss additional balls into the sequence gradually. Recommend that each player only concentrate on the person she tosses balls to, and the person she receives balls from. Challenge players to juggle a given number of balls as long as possible.

Diagram 6.5

Jugglemania

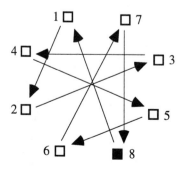

Chapter 7

Games for Large Groups

Large group games are the most complex, since the amount and variety of activity generally increases with the number of players in a game. Large groups most often contain 15 to 30 players, although *Raindrops* (p.121) may be played with as few as 8 players, and *Octopus* (p.122) with as many as 40 players. Games with as many as 30 or 40 players are recommended only when leaders are confident that all participants can have an active role.

Alignments are still more varied than with small group games, but movements and equipment utilized are not necessarily more complex. Since more large group games are competitive compared to partner and small group games, the social climate may be more intense. Leaders need to be aware of individual performances, because the skills of any given player are displayed in front of more peers. Leaders can then monitor peer responses to one another so players are built up, rather than torn down, through game experiences. Even if winning is not emphasized during large group games, the psychological maturity required is best suited to older elementary and middle school players. Still, primary level children can succeed in some of the activities, especially in settings where adults can participate with them.

(1) MUSICAL HOOPS

Description

Goals: Respect and trust others.
                 Practice rhythmical expression.

Alignment: Standing scattered on basketball or volleyball court,
                 depending on number of players.

Movements: Variety of locomotor skills.

Equipment: Boom box, music, one hoop for every three people.

Social   Cooperative.
  structure: 12-30 players, ages 5 to 8.

Directions

Scatter hoops evenly throughout the playing area. When the music begins, have players travel on their feet any way they choose without touching or stepping in a hoop. When the music stops, tell all players to get inside a hoop. The same hoop may have anywhere from zero to several players, as long as everyone is entirely inside some hoop (with whatever body parts touch the floor).

For each additional round remove one (10-20 players) or two (21-30 players) hoops. As the number of hoops decreases, encourage players to help each other and creatively maximize space inside remaining hoops. Score the game by how few hoops remain with all players still fitting inside.

Note: To maintain safety with larger groups, exclude running as one of the movement options.

Figure 7.1: Illustration of *Musical Hoops*.

(2) HEADS UP

Description

Goals:	Help others. Practice balancing.
Alignment:	Standing scattered throughout playing area.
Movements:	Balancing, squatting, walking.
Equipment:	One beanbag per person, markers to outline playing area.
Social structure:	Cooperative. 8-30 players, ages 5 to 8.

Directions

Give each player a beanbag to balance on his head or shoulder. On signal, instruct all players to walk within the playing area without letting the beanbag fall off. When a beanbag falls off someone's head, tell him to let it drop to the floor. Allow the person to resume play when someone else retrieves the beanbag and puts it back in place (while trying to maintain the position of his own beanbag). Score the game by monitoring the maximum length of time that all players have the beanbag intact. Each time a beanbag falls, begin monitoring time again.

Alternative: For additional challenge, require players to move in other ways while balancing the beanbags (i.e. have everyone travel sideways or gallop).

(3) RHYTHMICAL RED LIGHT

Description

Goals:	Respect and trust partner. Move at different tempos. Stop quickly under control.
Alignment:	Standing with partner inside hoop at one end of playing area.
Movements:	Balancing, choice of locomotion.
Equipment:	Drum and beater, four markers to indicate scoring lines.
Social structure:	Cooperative within competitive. 10-30 players, ages 5 to 8.

Directions

Have partners stand inside the hoop while holding it waist high. Designate a drummer to select a form of locomotion and to stand on the midline with her back to the group. Have the drummer hit the drum at whatever constant tempo she chooses. Challenge partners to advance at that tempo as far as possible before the drum stops. The drummer signals she is stopping with a loud drum beat, then turns around quickly to see if players are still moving their feet. (Other body parts may move.) Require anyone caught moving to start over. Have the drummer vary the form of locomotion and tempo of the drum in successive rounds. Suggest that the drummer also progress down the floor to remain ahead of all partners (indicated by arrow in Diagram 7.1). Award partners one point for getting to the "midline," and two points for getting to the endline. Give other players a turn playing the drum as time permits.

Diagram 7.1

Rhythmical Red Light

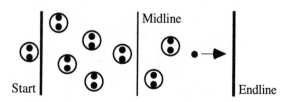

(4) SQUARE SOCCER

Description

Goals: Use kicking and trapping in game situation.

Alignment: Standing spread out on four sides of a square.

Movements: Kicking, trapping.

Equipment: One nerf soccer ball for every five people.

Social   Competitive.
  structure: 12-30 players, ages 5 to 8.

Directions

Have two teams each occupy two sides of a square, or four teams each occupy one side, as shown in Diagram 7.2. Instruct players to kick balls past any opponent's endline while preventing balls from passing their own endline. Award a point for each ball that goes beyond an endline below the waist. Allow players to trap or block balls with any body parts except hands and arms. Require teams to remain on or behind their kicking line. Rotate which teams begin with extra balls. With older players, use bouncier balls and allow use of the hands.

Diagram 7.2
Square Soccer

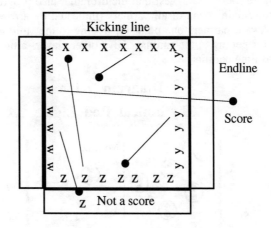

(5) DOUBLE DIRECTION KICKBALL

Description

Goals: Use fielding, throwing, and kicking in game situation.

Alignment: Half the players spread out in field; half the players
              waiting to kick.

Movements: Catching, fielding, kicking, running, throwing.

Equipment: Two different colored playground balls, four bases.

Social   Competitive.
 structure: 12-16 players, ages 5 to 8.

Directions

Kickers: Have two players kick at a time, with the balls resting on opposite sides of home plate. Instruct players to kick the ball between the baselines, but have fielders play any ball kicked forward. Have runners advance opposite directions around the bases, and award one point per base. If one of the balls is missed, have that player attempt another kick immediately (and keep trying until successful), and proceed around the bases slightly after the other kicker. Have all players kick before switching to the field, rather than recording outs.

Fielders: Tell players to retrieve the balls and get the corresponding colored ball to a base ahead of each runner. For example, if fielders pass a ball to first base while the clockwise runner is between second and first, award the runner two points for rounding third base and second base. Require fielders to advance balls by passing, rather than traveling with their bodies. Give the fielding team one point for each kicked ball caught on a fly, but have them attempt to stop that runner's progress in the same manner. Following each pair of kicks, rotate fielding positions.

(6) RABBIT IN THE HOLE

Description

Goals: Exercise total body intermittently.
                Practice dodging in game situation.

Alignment: Standing in groups of three, one person between the
                other two.

Movements: Dodging, running, tagging.

Equipment: None.

Social   Cooperative within competitive.
   structure: 15-30 players, ages 5 to 8.

Directions

Rabbit in the Hole originated in Peru. Arrange each group of three with
two people clasping hands to form a "tree," and one person standing in
the middle as the "rabbit" (R's in Diagram 7.3). Designate one group of
three as roving rabbits. Have roving rabbits stand on predetermined
markers spaced as far from trees as trees are from each other. On the
signal, instruct all trees to raise their branches, forcing rabbits to change
trees. At the same time, tell roving rabbits to attempt entering a tree.
Have trees lower their branches as soon as a rabbit enters, allowing only
one rabbit in a tree at a time. To increase challenge, repeat the signal at
more frequent intervals and/or require rabbits to move in particular ways
(i.e. galloping, hopping). Rotate positions until all players have been
rabbits.

Diagram 7.3
Rabbit in the Hole

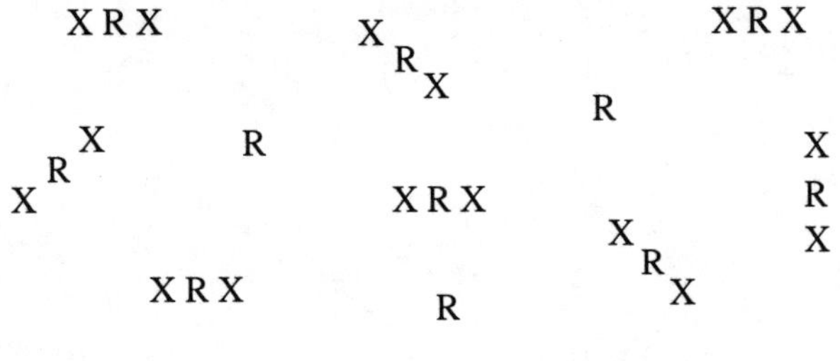

(7) RAINDROPS

Description

Goals:	Communicate with others.
	Practice striking one-handed.
Alignment:	Standing in a mass at close range.
Movements:	Striking one-handed.
Equipment:	One 10- to 12-inch balloon per person.
Social structure:	Cooperative.
	8-30 players, ages 5 to 9.

Directions

Instruct all players to strike their balloons, or "raindrops" vertically into the air. Then have players strike other balloons into the air without hitting the same balloon twice in succession. Require players to leave balloons on the floor once they land. End the game when there are half as many balloons as there are people.

Alternatives: For additional challenge, prevent players from hitting the same color balloon twice in succession. For still more challenge, prevent players from using their hands to strike the balloons after the initial vertical hit.

(8) OCTOPUS

Description

Goals:	Exercise total body intermittently.
	Practice dodging.
Alignment:	Standing on one endline facing the other endline.
Movements:	Dodging, running, tagging.
Equipment:	Markers to outline playing area; the larger the group, the larger the area.
Social structure:	Cooperative within competitive.
	16-40 players, ages 5 to 12.

Directions

Octopus originated in Canada. Designate two taggers, or "octopi" to stand in the center of the area facing the group. Have the taggers yell "octopus," then instruct players to run from one endline to the other without being tagged. Have players who are tagged stop in that place and become additional octopi. Consider players who leave the area as tagged at the point of infraction. During ensuing rounds, have tagged octopi catch remaining runners by reaching with their hands. Do not allow tagged octopi to move their feet, except to alternate the direction faced. With more than 25 players, begin the game with three roving octopi.

Alternative: To challenge intermediate level children more, instruct players to travel in pairs with joined hands or linked elbows, including the original octopi. Consider partners who separate as tagged at the point of infraction. Tagged octopi remain joined and tag others from that location with their free hands. If the original octopi separate, require them to rejoin before tagging more people. With an odd number of runners, begin the game with one group of three people.

(9) AROUND THE HORN

Description

Goals: Practice kicking, throwing, and catching.

Alignment: Half the players spread out in field; half the players
                 waiting to kick.

Movements: Batting, catching, kicking, punting, running, throwing
                 overhand.

Equipment: Kickball, four bases.

Social   Cooperative within competitive.
    structure: 12-20 players, ages 7 to 10.

Directions

Kickers: Have players count off to determine kicking order. Have the
first player choose to kick a rolled ball from the pitcher or punt the ball
into fair territory. If the player does not kick a fair ball twice in a row,
require him to choose the other option for kicking the ball until it is
fair. Following the fair kick, instruct all players on the kicking team
to run in order around the bases as far as possible. Score one run for
each player who passes third base. Allow half the players on a team to
kick before switching to the field, rather than recording outs.

Fielders: Have players retrieve the kicked ball and return it to the pitcher
to stop the runners' scoring. Require fielders to advance the ball by
passing it to four different teammates (six teammates with 16-20
players). Have the last pass go to the pitcher. One possible passing
sequence is indicated by numbers in Diagram 7.4. Do not count the
player who retrieves the ball as one of the passes, and do not allow
players to travel while holding the ball. Following each kick, rotate
fielding positions in the order indicated by letters in the diagram.

Alternative: To increase scoring, eliminate second base. For variety,
substitute batting for kicking. In this case, have players choose to bat
a pitched ball or toss the ball to themselves. Also allow players to
choose from two different sizes of bats and balls.

Diagram 7.4
Around the Horn

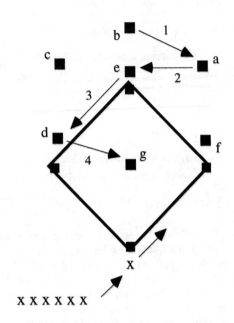

(10) SPOT BALL

Description

Goals:	Practice throwing and catching. Practice agility running.
Alignment:	Striking team standing in three lines behind the endline of a basketball court; fielding team standing on "spots" scattered behind the midline of the court.
Movements:	Catching, running, striking one-handed, throwing overhand, tossing underhand.
Equipment:	Soft, pliable ball, enough carpet squares or other spots for one team.
Social structure:	Cooperative within competitive. 15-30 players, ages 7 to 11.

Directions

Striking team: Have the first person in the middle line strike the ball out of her hand so it crosses the quarterline. Tell the first runner in the other two lines to run around the nearest marker and back across the endline. If a marker is knocked down or misplaced, require the runner to replace it before continuing on. Have runners continue rounding their markers in order until the fielding team completes their tasks. Tell runners they may run more than one time. Award a point for each time a runner rounds a marker and returns to the endline. Have each player in the middle line strike the ball before switching to the field.

Fielding team: While the batting team rounds markers, instruct the fielding team to complete six throws and catches without dropping the ball. The sequence of catches numbered in Diagram 7.5 indicates an extra throw because one was dropped (dotted line). Do not allow the same player to receive the ball twice during the same turn. Require players to have at least one foot on their spots to throw or catch the ball. After fielders complete passes, tell them to change to a different spot for the next turn. Blow a whistle when fielders have changed spots to end the strikers' scoring for that turn. Have runners in process become the first runner for the next turn. As time permits, rotate players to the striking line for future innings.

Diagram 7.5

Spot Ball

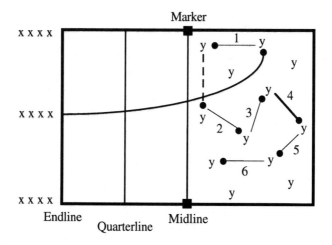

(11) ALIVE AND KICKIN'

Description

Goals: Respect other people's spaces.
                Practice reacting to ball quickly.

Alignment: Lying down in a circle facing the center.

Movements: Kicking two-footed, pushing.

Equipment: 36- or 48-inch beach ball.

Social   Cooperative.
  structure: 9-15 players, ages 7 to 11.

Directions

Designate one "rover" for every three players. Instruct all players
except the rovers to hold hands and form a circle. Have circle players
drop hands and lay down on their backs with their feet toward the center,
lifted off the floor. Tell rovers to stand outside the circle, facing the
center. Toss the beach ball toward the feet of the circle players.
Challenge circle players to keep the ball "alive" by kicking it as many
times as possible. When the ball leaves the circle, have rovers hit or
push it back toward a kicker to continue the sequence. Award one point
for each consecutive kick without letting the ball land on the floor or
stop. Rotate rovers as time allows.

Note: Have circle players remove eye glasses to avoid possible injury.

Alternative: If the kicks of the group are difficult to count, score the
game based on time by monitoring how long the ball remains moving
off the floor.

(12) BUWAN-BUWAN

Description

Goals: Exercise total body intermittently.

Alignment: Standing scattered inside 20-foot diameter circle.

Movements: Dodging, running, tagging.

Equipment: None.

Social
    structure: Competitive.
               14-20 players, ages 7 to 11.

Directions

Buwan-Buwan originated in the Philippines. Designate two taggers to stand anywhere on the circle. Have the other players, or runners spread out inside the circle. Instruct taggers to catch a runner, while remaining on the circumference of the circle, or on one of the diameters depicted in Diagram 7.6. When a runner is tagged, have him change roles with that tagger. If a minute lapses without a change, designate two new taggers.

Diagram 7.6

Buwan-Buwan

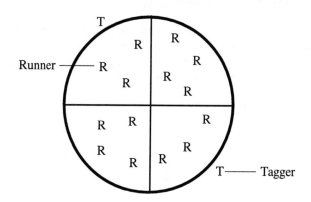

(13) CATCH A TAIL

Description

Goals: Respect and trust others.
                Utilize dodging in game situation.

Alignment: Standing in chains scattered on half or entire volleyball
                court, depending on number of players.

Movements: Dodging, grasping, running.

Equipment: One handkerchief per group, markers to outline playing
                area.

Social   Cooperative within competitive.
   structure: 4-5 players per chain (3-6 chains), ages 7 to 12.

Directions

Catch a Tail originated in Nigeria. Instruct players in each group to
form a chain by standing in a straight line and grasping onto each
other's waists (not belt loops). Have the last person in each chain wear
a handkerchief, or "tail" tucked into the back of her pants. Instruct
players to tuck in only a small part of the cloths so others may see
them easily. On signal, have each group maneuver so the first player
in line can grab the tail of any other chain. Tell lead players to hang
onto seized tails, while trying to grab more tails. When a group loses
their tail, allow them to continue seizing other tails until the end of the
round, rather than eliminating a group.

When possible, stop rounds when one group still has their tail intact.
Award two points to this group. Give one point to groups for each tail
seized. Subtract one point for each time a group steps out of bounds or
breaks apart (may result in a negative score).

Figure 7.2: Illustration of *Catch a Tail*.

(14) CHAIN TAG

Description

Goals: Respect and trust others.
Exercise total body continuously.

Alignment: Standing with chains equally spaced (in rectangle or square formation), facing center of playing area.

Movements: Dodging, running, tagging.

Equipment: Hoop (if center circle is not available), markers to outline playing area.

Social
structure: Cooperative within competitive.
3-5 players per chain (3-6 chains), ages 7 to 14.

Directions

Designate a tagger to stand in the center circle, and arrange chains in the manner depicted by Line a in Diagram 7.7. On signal, allow chains to move anywhere in the boundaries, without separating and without forming a closed chain or circle. Allow any other shape in order to protect ends of chains. Possible shapes are depicted by Lines b, c and d in the diagram. Have the tagger try to tag an end person of any chain and return to the circle. Then have the tagger try to repeat this procedure as often as possible in 60 seconds (by tagging the same player or different ends of chains). Award the tagger one point for each time (a) an end person is tagged, (b) a chain comes apart, or (c) a chain steps out of bounds (any one of its players). Appoint several players to be tagger as time permits. Each time taggers switch, rotate different players to the ends of chains.

Note: The younger the players, the shorter the chains need to be.

Alternatives: Extend the time limit to 90 seconds to encourage more exercise and more scoring. In addition, appoint two taggers at a time with five or six chains in the game.

Diagram 7.7

Chain Tag

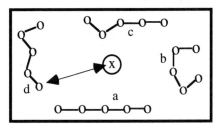

(15) FLAG TAG

Description

Goals: Exercise total body continuously.
Move in relation to others safely.

Alignment: Standing scattered on basketball or volleyball court, depending on number of players.

Movements: Dodging, grabbing, running, tagging.

Equipment: Markers to outline playing area, one nylon belt with two flags per person.

Social
  structure: Competitive.
             8-30 players, ages 7 to 14.

Directions

Give all players a belt with two flags to wear so flags can be easily seen (not covered with hand or clothing). On signal, tell all players to grab flags from the belts of other players. If someone leaves the boundaries, have him give a flag to the nearest player. When a player loses both flags, allow him to remain in the game to grab other flags. Stop the game while several players still have at least one flag. Award one point for each flag grabbed from opponent's belts, and two points for each flag remaining on a person's belt.

Alternative: For variety, play the game with two to four teams using different colored flags.

(16) EVERYBODY IT

Description

Goals: Exercise total body intermittently.
                 Move in relation to others safely.

Alignment: Standing scattered on basketball or volleyball court,
                 depending on number of players.

Movements: Dodging, running, sliding, tagging.

Equipment: Markers to outline playing area.

Social   Competitive.
  structure: 8-30 players, ages 7 to 14.

Directions

On signal, tell all players to tag one another. Have tagged players sit
down in that place, but continue tagging. Require sitting players to
cross their legs and maintain an upright posture to avoid being stepped
on or tripping others. If players tag one another simultaneously, or are
unsure who tagged first, have both players sit down. Have players who
step outside the boundaries sit down at the place they crossed the line.

Alternative: For additional challenge, require standing players to tag
with their nondominant hands only.

(17) SCATTER DODGEBALL

Description

Goals: Practice throwing two-handed.
                 Exercise total body intermittently.

Alignment: Standing on perimeter of basketball or volleyball court.

Movements: Catching, dodging, running, throwing two-handed.

Equipment: One 6- to 8-inch playground or plastic ball for every six
                 people, markers to outline playing area.

Social   Competitive.
  structure: 8-30 players, ages 7 to 14.

Directions

Place the balls in the middle of the playing area. On signal, instruct most players to scatter, while the rest dart for a ball. Tell players with balls to hit others below the shoulders using a two-hand throw. Do not allow players who initially retrieve a ball to hit each other. Allow players to have only one ball at a time, and to take only one step while holding a ball (unlimited steps without ball). When someone is hit on a fly, or when a person's throw is caught on a fly, she sits down with legs crossed in that location. Allow players to stand up again under two conditions:

1. When the player who hit her sits down (if known).
2. When a stray ball comes within reach (while still sitting).

Score the game by the number of players each individual hits, or by which players are standing when time expires.

Alternative: For variety, scatter two to four teams throughout the area, having each team try to hit the other team's players (wearing different colored pinnies).

(18) PIN SOCCER

Description

Goals:	Use kicking and trapping in game situation. Practice kicking and passing accuracy.
Alignment:	Standing on two sides of playing area in three designated groups.
Movements:	Guarding, kicking, passing, trapping.
Equipment:	One youth soccer ball for every four people, six or eight pins, two different colored jerseys (one per person).
Social structure:	Competitive. 12-24 players, ages 8 to 12.

Directions

To the extent possible, divide players into three equal groups within each team. Have goalies stand near the pins, halfbacks stand near the midline on their defensive side, and forwards stand around the perimeter on their offensive side. Require goalies to remain outside the tires surrounding the pins, and forwards to remain between the slash marks shown in Diagram 7.8. Have halfbacks begin with the balls.

On signal, instruct halfbacks and forwards to kick down pins of the opponent. Award one point for each pin that falls, even if the opponent knocks one over accidentally. Each time a pin falls, tell that team to reset it immediately so it may be knocked down again. Scoring is more likely when players pass the ball, as illustrated in the diagram with arrows. At the end of each five minute period, combine player's individual points and rotate them to new positions. Switch goalies to halfbacks, halfbacks to forwards and forwards to goalies.

Diagram 7.8

Pin Soccer

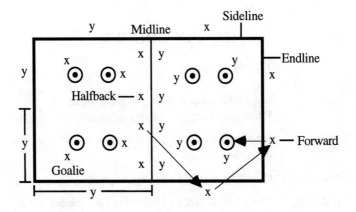

(19) GARBAGE BALL

Description

Goals:

Practice throwing overhand and catching.
Practice guarding opponent.

Alignment:

Each of four teams standing on their respective sides of a square, facing the center; Player 1 from each line standing in the scoring zone opposite her line, holding a ball; Player 2 standing in the defensive zone to her left.

Movements: Catching, guarding, throwing overhand.

Equipment: Eight 6-inch rubber balls, large garbage can, four different colored pinnies.

Social
structure:

Competitive.
20-32 players, ages 8 to 12.

Directions

Give each player in a scoring zone a ball. Tell her to make as many baskets as possible in a given round. Require players to catch a ball thrown from their team's endline on a fly, before attempting a basket with that same ball (indicated for Team W in Diagram 7.9). Have a player who acquires a ball in any other manner (even the start of the game) first throw it to her endline so it may be thrown back. Encourage players in the defensive and scoring zones to intercept an opponent's pass, as long as they remain in their respective zones. When a basket is made, leave the ball in the garbage can until the end of the round. Each time a ball lands in the garbage can, throw in a new ball to the player that made the basket (until all 10 balls have entered the game). End a round when eight baskets have been made. Following each round, rotate players clockwise.

Diagram 7.9
Garbage Ball

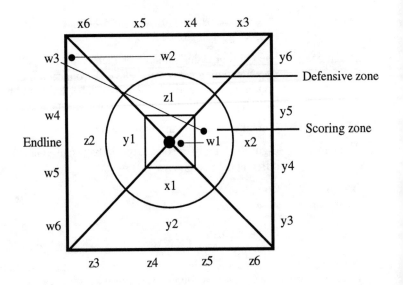

(20) SIDELINE BASKETBALL

Description

Goals:	Practice basketball skills in game situation.
	Exercise total body intermittently.
Alignment:	8-14 players standing on sideline; 6-10 players on court.
Movements:	Guarding, passing, shooting.
Equipment:	Two youth size basketballs.
Social structure:	Competitive.
	14-24 players, ages 8 to 12.

Directions

Give each team a basketball behind its own endline. Instruct teams to advance the ball up the court to score. Allow the ball to be advanced by passing only. Permit the ball to be passed to sideline and endline players, but not three times consecutively. (Refer to Diagram 7.10.) Require sideline and endline players to remain behind their lines. Keep play continuous by (a) having the closest sideline player immediately inbound a ball that leaves the boundaries, and (b) having the opposite endline player immediately inbound a ball following a basket. Following traveling and other violations, give the ball to the other team's closest sideline player. Rotate different sideline and endline players onto the court every five minutes.

Diagram 7.10

Sideline Basketball

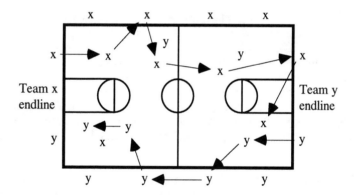

(21) FLAG QUEST

Description

Goals: Exercise total body intermittently.
Practice dodging.

Alignment: Standing scattered on two sides of playing area.

Movements: Dodging, grabbing, guarding, running, tagging.

Equipment: Markers to outline playing area, one pinney per person (two different colors), two "flags" (pinnies) and bicycle tires per team.

Social
  structure: Competitive.
              16-30 players, ages 8 to 14.

Directions

Give teams two flags to place inside bicycle tires on their respective sides (represented by different sized circles in Diagram 7.11). Locate tires one-third of the distance from each sideline, and one-third of the distance from endlines to the midline. Assign two players on each team to guard the flags without stepping inside or on a tire. On signal, instruct players to seize the other team's flags. Award one point for successfully grabbing a flag, and an additional point if the flag is brought back to the opponent's side without being tagged. Encourage players to seize flags again after being returned to their original location.

When players are tagged, have them go to that team's jail. Locate jails at the back center of each side, just out of bounds. Have players line up in jail in the order tagged, so they may leave jail in the same order. A jail break occurs when a player runs past the other team's endline without being tagged, as indicated by the arrow in the diagram. Allow the person from jail and the rescuer to return to their side outside the boundaries. Do not allow a player who crosses an endline to turn back for a flag, instead of rescuing a teammate. If a player crosses an endline and no teammates remain in jail, have the player go back to his side outside the boundaries.

Alternative: For variety, play the game in an outdoor setting with trees, buildings and/or other visual barriers.

Diagram 7.11
Flag Quest

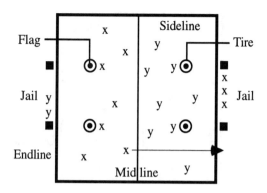

(22) FRISBEE FRAME

Description

Goals:	Practice throwing and catching.
Alignment:	Standing scattered in each of four squares.
Movements:	Catching, throwing one-handed.
Equipment:	One frisbee for every four players, 16 bicycle tires, markers to outline playing area.
Social structure:	Competitive. 16-32 players, ages 8 to 14.

Directions

Disperse frisbees equally throughout quadrants. On signal, instruct players to throw frisbees into other quadrants so they touch the ground before being caught (indicated by arrows in Diagram 7.12). Allow frisbees to be caught anywhere within a given team's quadrant, but require them to be thrown from within one of the team's bicycle tires. Have the closest team retrieve frisbees that land out of bounds. Award one point for each successful throw and one point for each fly caught. Have each player monitor her points and add them to the team total.

Diagram 7.12
Frisbee Frame

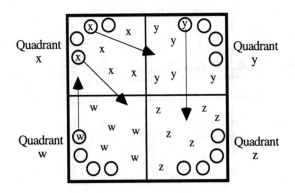

(23) DRIBBLE TAG

Description

Goals: Practice positioning body.
                     Practice dribbling.

Alignment: Standing scattered inside one-third of basketball court.

Movements: Dodging, dribbling.

Equipment: Markers to divide area into three sections, one
                     child or youth size soccer ball per person.

Social   Competitive.
    structure: 8-30 players, ages 8 to 14.

Directions

On signal, instruct players to dribble a ball in one third of the court,
labeled Area a in Diagram 7.13. At the same time, challenge players to
kick other balls outside that area. Have anyone whose ball leaves Area
a, retrieve it and enter Area b. If a player's ball is kicked out of Area b,
have that player enter a third game in Area c. If a player's ball is kicked
out of Area c, tell him to retrieve it and continue playing in that area.
Begin another round when no players remain in Area a.

Alternative: For variety, play the game dribbling with hands, instead of with feet, substituting a basketball for the soccer ball. In this case, advance a player to the next area if he loses control of the dribble, even if the ball does not leave the area.

Diagram 7.13

Dribble Tag

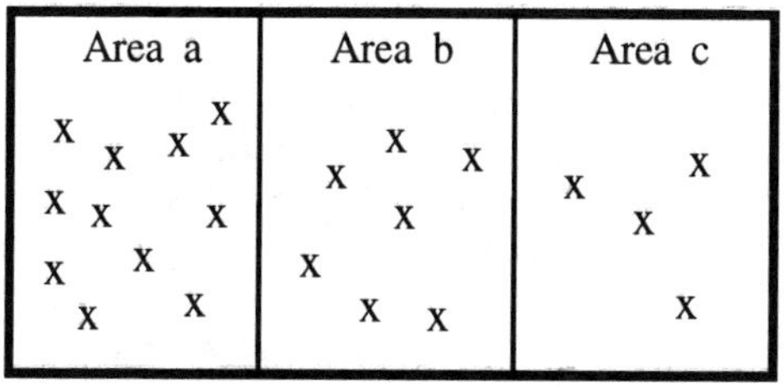

Area a	Area b	Area c

X   X
  X X
X X   X
X X
 X   X
	X
	 X X X
	X
	 X
	X
	 X X
		X
		X
		  X
		
		   X

(24) LINK BALL

Description

Goals:	Respect and trust others. Practice throwing and catching. Practice dodging.
Alignment:	Standing scattered equally on each half of the playing area.
Movements:	Catching, dodging, throwing one-handed.
Equipment:	One 8-inch nerf ball for every four people, markers to designate midline and outside boundaries.
Social structure:	Cooperative within competitive. 15-30 players, ages 9 to 14.

Directions

Instruct players to hit opponents using a one-hand throw. Have a player who is hit on a fly, or whose throw is caught on a fly, become a shagger in her end zone. Tell shaggers to retrieve loose balls and give them to teammates without leaving the end zone, as shown in Diagram 7.14. When a second player enters the same end zone, have teammates link elbows together and return to the throwing area (likewise with the third and fourth players).

Have linked players continue throwing and catching balls using their outside arms, but allow them to travel anywhere in the playing area, even across the midline. When one of the linked players is hit by a fly ball, or throws a ball that is caught, require that pair to return to the end zone to get different partners. No more than two people will remain in the end zone at a given time. End the game when all players from one team are either linked or in their end zone.

Diagram 7.14

Link Ball

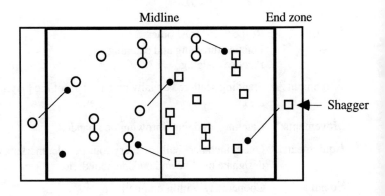

(25) MOSQUITO

Description

Goals: Exercise total body intermittently.
                Move in relation to others safely.

Alignment: Standing scattered on basketball or volleyball court,
                depending on number of players.

Movements: Dodging, running, sliding, tagging.

Equipment: Markers to outline playing area.

Social   Competitive.
  structure: 8-30 players, ages 9 to 14.

Directions

Mosquito originated in the Philippines under the name *Hospital Tag*. The name is changed so players are not encouraged to "wound" one another. On signal, instruct all players, or "mosquitos" to "bite" each other with a tag (as in the game *Everybody It*, p.132). The first time a player is tagged, have him hold one hand on the spot bitten (as if slapping a mosquito) and continue traveling and tagging people with the other hand. The second time the same player is tagged, have him hold a hand on the second spot bitten (releasing the first hand) and continue traveling and tagging others. The third time a player is tagged, tell him to leave the boundaries and do any exercise (i.e. jumping jacks, sit-ups) until the round is over. Regard simultaneous tagging as a tagging incident for both players. End the game when one-fourth the number of players remains untagged.

Games for Success

(26) QUADRANT BALL

Description

Goals: Practice throwing and catching.
       Use peripheral vision.

Alignment: Each group standing on its endline.

Movements: Catching, dodging, throwing one-handed.

Equipment: Markers to outline four squares and end zones, one
         8-inch nerf ball for every four players, pinnies of four
         different colors (one per person).

Social   Competitive.
   structure: 16-32 players, ages 9 to 14.

Directions

Have players get balls from the middle of each square and try to hit people on other teams. Limit players to one ball at a time, and one step while holding a ball (unlimited steps without ball). When someone is hit on a fly, or when her throw is caught on a fly, have the player go to the end zone diagonally opposite her square without cutting through another square. (See dotted line in Diagram 7.15.) Encourage end zone players to continue throwing at opponents as they acquire stray balls, depicted by Team Z in the diagram. If an end zone player catches a ball on a fly (usually from teammate), have the player return to her square without cutting through other squares. Allow end zone players to retrieve balls that leave the back of the end zone, providing they return before throwing the ball. Challenge teams to have the most people in their squares when time expires. When time expires, have players complete transitions to and from end zones before counting points.

Diagram 7.15
Quadrant Ball

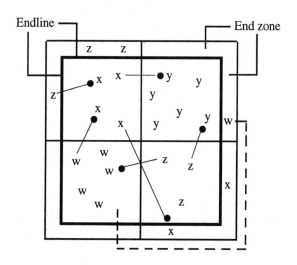

Endline — | — End zone

(27) VIKING'S SHORE PATROL

Description

Goals:	Exercise total body intermittently.
	Understand role of smuggler in Viking England culture.
Alignment:	Half the players standing inside perimeter of area; half the players standing outside perimeter.
Movements:	Dodging, running, tagging.
Equipment:	Handkerchief, two different colored pinnies.
Social structure:	Competitive.
	10-24 players, ages 9 to 14.

Directions

Vikings Shore Patrol originated in England. Have smugglers determine a player to secretly hide the handkerchief ("goods") on himself, and one player to be captain. Spread out smugglers outside the Viking's "shore," or territory. Spread out Vikings inside the territory, with one person guarding the hiding place (without entering it). Challenge the smugglers to get the goods to the hiding place to avoid a customs tax. Designate smugglers who are tagged by a Viking inside the territory as spies. Designate Vikings who are tagged by the captain inside the territory as spies also. Tell spies to leave the territory and give verbal directions to respective teammates. Immunize the guard and captain ("G" and "C" in Diagram 7.16) from being tagged and do not have them wear pinnies to distinguish them from other players.

Award the Vikings a point for tagging the smuggler with the goods before the goods reach the hiding place. Award the smugglers a point if the player with the handkerchief sets it in the hiding place before being tagged. Play two or three rounds. Then have teams change roles whether or not a score has occurred.

Alternatives: For variety, play the game in an outdoor setting with trees, buildings and/or other visual barriers. Also try having two smugglers carry goods with larger groups.

Diagram 7.16
Viking's Shore Patrol

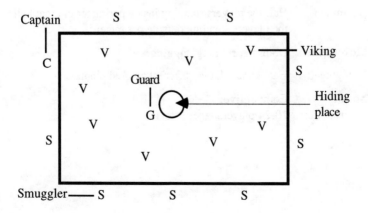

(28) ONE-CATCH VOLLEYBALL

Description

Goals: Practice striking.
                        Improve hand-eye coordination.

Alignment: Standing in rows on two sides of volleyball court.

Movements: Striking one- and two-handed.

Equipment: Youth, or oversize volleyball.

Social   Competitive.
  structure: 8-16 players, ages 10 to 13.

Directions

Have players begin with an underhand serve. From then on, require teams to touch the ball three times, or the ball goes to the other team. Each time the ball crosses the net, have the first player catch it and toss it in the air on her side of the net. Require the second and third players to hit the ball as in volleyball, with the third contact sending the ball over the net. Each time either team earns a side out, have both teams rotate clockwise.

Alternatives: For variety, allow one bounce per side instead of one catch. To provide more challenge for middle school age players, use a regulation volleyball.

(29) ARANGA TOUCH

Description

Goals: Practice throwing and catching in game situation.
                 Exercise total body intermittently.

Alignment: Standing scattered on basketball court; catchers and
                 defenders at opposite ends outside court.

Movements: Catching, dodging, guarding, throwing.

Equipment: One playground ball or football.

Social   Competitive.
  structure: 10-18 players, ages 10-13.

Directions

Aranga Touch originated in New Zealand. Position a catcher from one team and a defender from the other team in each end zone beyond the respective endlines of a basketball court. Instruct each team to advance the ball to its end zone and complete a pass to the catcher. Award one point for each completion. Require players to advance the ball by passing only, allowing one step in any direction. Disallow passes longer than half the length of the court. Encourage teams to prevent the opponent from scoring by intercepting or knocking down passes. When a ball is dropped or thrown out of bounds, have the other team put it in play at that location uncontested. Following a score or incomplete pass in an end zone, have the other team's defender put the ball in play uncontested. Rotate which players serve as catchers and defenders as time allows.

Alternatives: For additional challenge, add a second ball to the game. If players are too congested around the balls, restrict half of each team's players to each half of the court.

(30) ORBIT

Description

Goals:	Respect other people's spaces.
	Practice reacting to ball quickly.
Alignment:	Half the players resting on their backs in a circle facing the center; half the players standing outside the circle facing the center.
Movements:	Balancing, kicking two-footed, pushing.
Equipment:	36- or 48-inch cage ball, one spot or carpet square for every two people.
Social structure:	Competitive.
	12-20 players, ages 10 to 14.

Directions

Stand half the players on a circle (or on a circle of individual markers). Rest half the players on their backs, lifting feet off the floor. Toss the ball toward the feet of the resting players. Award resting players a point every time they kick the ball "into orbit" outside the circle of standing players, as indicated in Diagram 7.17. Challenge standing players to restrain the ball, while keeping at least one foot on their circle or markers. Award standing players a point every time the ball touches the floor inside the circle of resting players. When the ball lands on the floor in the neutral zone, have the nearest standing player toss it back into play. Make the neutral zone and inner circle smaller or larger to allow more or less scoring, respectively. Reverse roles of teams every five minutes.

Note: Have resting players remove eye glasses and keep their heads on the floor to avoid possible injury.

Diagram 7.17
Orbit

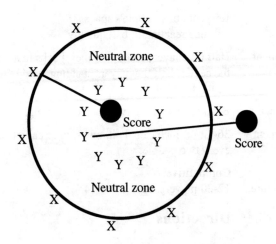

Chapter 8

Administering Games

This book is devoted to the subject of game content and ways to administer game content so all children may be included. In a sense, game administration involves monitoring game elements, one of the topics discussed in chapter 2. Other responsibilities associated with game administration are more peripheral than monitoring game elements. This chapter addresses some "how to's" of selected peripheral responsibilities that occur before, during, or following a game.

Pregame Responsibilities

Pregame responsibilities include setting up a game, determining groups, and explaining the game. Each of these responsibilities may be carried out effectively if leaders have first planned well. Planning involves familiarizing oneself with games in advance, and selecting games that are developmentally appropriate for a particular group of players. Leaders also need to familiarize themselves with the recreational facility and space available. Aspects of the physical space often suggest safety considerations and how to best set up a game.

Setting up Game

Games requiring set up may be prepared by a leader, or by capable children under the direction of a leader. Set up most often involves laying out boundaries and organizing equipment for tasks involving locomotion, nonlocomotion, object control or sport skills. Setting up a game before a group arrives maximizes playing time and achieves better organization and control. When a large group needs to wait for a game to be set up, some children fill their time by bothering others. Sometimes leaders may want to share responsibility for setting up with children, even when games cannot be set up in advance. The longer the game time allotted, the more leaders can sacrifice a few minutes to let children help.

Determining Groups

Groups should be determined in a way that does not single out players. Instead of choosing players with captains, leaders may use arbitrary criteria. The most common arbitrary criteria is to have children "count off," using one number for each group needed. So, if four groups are needed, children count from one through four until all receive a number. Leaders need to be sure children do not intentionally change their position in line to receive a particular number.

Other criteria for determining groups include birth dates (by month), eye color, or number of letters in the last name. When selected criteria do not evenly determine groups, a leader may ask a couple of children to change groups. When this occurs, children are not singled out by ability, since they know any child could be asked to change.

In partner games, leaders may encourage children to find a partner of equal ability. The following guideline helps include all players: "If someone asks you to be a partner, the answer is always yes." Then if one or two children have not found partners after a short while, the leader may quietly assign children so no one is left wandering around.

The impact of a child's participation on a particular team is lessened when leaders rotate players regularly. Some games require regular rotation, such as *Link Ball* (p.141) and *Advantage* (p.110). Other times leaders may rotate players during the same activity or in between activities. In a partner game, children could play one round with an initial partner, and successive rounds with different partners. In an activity involving more than two teams, a given team may face different opponents. In addition to rotating opponents, leaders are encouraged to change the make up of teams so a given team does not always win or lose.

Explaining Game

When explaining games, initial comments should cover the most critical aspects only. Then children may begin moving without a long delay. Critical aspects of a game include the main goal(s), primary rules and safety considerations.

Leaders cannot assume children understand the goal(s) of a game. Leaders often alert players to motor skills or scoring strategies involved in a game, yet assume players will cooperate without specific directions. Cooperative skills, such as helping others and communicating respectfully, need to be directly taught in the same manner as other game skills. Deline (1991) and Hellison (1987) remind us that children are often uncooperative because they lack specific skills, not because they lack desire to cooperate. One way to teach cooperative skills, is by assigning roles to various group members. Glover and Midura (1992) suggest the roles of organizer, praiser, encourager, summarizer and recorder (pp.14-15). Naturally, the roles may be changed to fit a particular activity. A leader may wish to assign a conflict manager for one activity and forego the role of recorder. After assigning group roles, the leader can monitor children's interaction and intervene when children need a particular role modeled.

In addition to the goal(s) of a game, children need to know primary rules and safety considerations before playing. The more complex a game, the more the initial explanation should include "chalk talk" or "walk through" examples. Children more fully understand positioning of players and options with equipment when they see, as well as hear, examples. A chalk talk is a way to visually diagram game information in a short time. A walk through example requires more time, but is more concrete than a chalk talk, because selected players physically model aspects of the game.

After leaders have explained primary rules and safety considerations of a game, children can play briefly to determine what they understand. Then secondary rules can be added and children can ask further questions. A primary rule for *Scatter Dodgeball* (p.132) is to hit other players below the shoulders to insure safety. By contrast, not allowing players to have more than one ball at a time is a secondary rule, since the information is not necessary for people to initially try the game.

Game Responsibilities

Game responsibilities occur after an activity is under way. Key responsibilities include monitoring time, refereeing and encouraging children.

Monitoring Time

Monitoring time is a responsibility closely linked to including all children in a game. If time expires before all players get to perform some skill, those who did not get a turn feel cheated. In *Kickball*, for instance, everyone needs a chance to kick the ball because kicking is the central skill in the game. In some games, however, time does not permit each child to perform the central skill, or several skills are incorporated to equal degrees. In these cases, all children do not necessarily need to perform all skills. An example of the former occurs in *Rhythmical Red Light* (p.117). If each child takes a turn beating the drum, a group of 20 children will require about 60 minutes to play the game. *Let My People Go* (p.56) provides an example of the latter. Since playing the role of a Moses or Pharoah provides equal involvement, players do not need to serve in both capacities.

Modifying rules helps a leader conserve time. To insure all children kick the ball in *Kickball*, leaders may have each player on a team kick before switching that team to the field. Eliminating the three outs saves transition time required to switch teams, since teams switch less frequently. An additional benefit is that a player's out does not cause his team to switch to the field. Kicking and fielding opportunities may be increased further by utilizing two kickers at a time, as in *Double Direction Kickball* (p.119). Two kickers are involved by running opposite directions around the bases, and fielders, therefore, gain twice the chances to catch and throw the ball.

Another important aspect of monitoring time involves stoppage of play. A leader may wonder how long children need to play a game to achieve the goals. Two general principles are to (a) provide variety by playing more than one game, and (b) stop a game when interest is high. Whether or not these principles may be accomplished depends on the game. *Flag Quest* (p.138) is designed as an ongoing game with considerable strategy. The strategy normally takes children at least 20 minutes to understand and implement. By contrast, one round of *Everybody It* (p.132) requires only about 45 seconds. Therefore, *Flag Quest* would probably require the entire time allotted, whereas *Everybody It* could be played several times, and still move on to one or two other games. Another factor determining game length is familiarity. On the average, unfamiliar games take longer than familiar games because more time for explanation is required. Therefore, leaders would be better off to play one familiar and one unfamiliar game on the same day, rather than attempting two new games.

Refereeing

Refereeing is best done by children as they play so the game leader is free to observe and comment as needed. A second reason for helping children referee their own games is that adults will not always be present when children play. Since play occurs during recess and at home when adults do not immediately oversee the activity, children need practice interpreting rules and settling problems.

A third reason for having children referee their own games is to develop character (as discussed in chapter 4). Even if adults were always available to settle problems among children, this is not in the best interests of helping children mature. For children to act as responsible adults they need to assume increasing responsibility for interacting with peers and making decisions. Adults can guide them in this process by helping them distinguish between a respectful and a disrespectful response to a coach, or between an encouraging and discouraging response to a teammate.

Naturally, refereeing one's own games is a developmental process. Children cannot just be thrown into an activity and be told to referee fairly. They need modeling by adults and specific guidelines for making decisions. Some guidelines come in the form of biblical principles. Chapter 4 suggests several examples of biblical principles to incorporate into games. Without singling out individuals publicly, leaders can appeal to children to sacrifice their pride or other personal desire to rule in favor of an opponent. Solving problems in this manner takes time. A leader may wish to balance this problem solving approach with expedient problem solving. If children take time to work through each little dispute the flow of the game is interrupted too often. Expedient solutions can be built right into game rules so the leader does not necessarily need to intervene. In tagging games, for example, the tagger can simply decide whether or not another player was actually tagged. The concrete guideline gives children opportunities to be trustworthy and reduces the tendency for arguing.

Encouraging Children

Leaders need to carefully observe a game to determine what kind of experience children are having. Careful observation involves seeing all aspects of a game, and not just intense activity surrounding the ball or other equipment. Chapter 2 suggests ways to modify games based on what occurs. Whether or not a leader actually changes a game, the leader has an important role as an encourager. Giving encouragement affirms children for accomplishing some aspect of a game.

Many examples of affirmative responses are given in Table 8.1. Items 1 through 32 are general superlatives that potentially motivate or excite children. Leaders are encouraged to give more specific information when time permits. A leader may wish to affirm skill performance (Items 34-38), strategy (Items 39-41), attitude (Items 42-44), or effort (Items 45-49). Using a wide variety of responses helps children receive comments more sincerely. In addition to affirming children, leaders may wish to correct a child's performance, or suggest what they can do differently. Corrections tend to carry a negative connotation, since they emphasize what a child did not do in the past, rather than what the child can do in the future:

> Correction: "You didn't get under the ball far enough."
> Suggestion: "Try to get under the ball a little farther."

Corrections and suggestions tend to be received better when they follow affirmations:

> Affirmation: "Nice hustle getting to the ball."
> Suggestion: "Next time see if you can also get under it more."

Even when leaders give children a lot of affirmative responses, they need to guard against sending hidden messages. Items 50 through 53 in Figure 8.1 provide examples of hidden messages. Hidden messages may (a) encourage pursuing an unrealistic goal, (b) focus on a child's personhood, (c) be misdirected, or (d) be sarcastic.

An unrealistic goal is represented by Item 50. If a child really believes enough practice leads to perfection, the child may also believe anything less than perfection is unacceptable. Item 51 refers to a child's personhood, rather than her performance. Even though the response is positive, it incorrectly suggests a person's character changes with her performance. A misdirected response is represented by Item 52. The focus is on what the performance is not (bad), instead of on what the performance is (good). A child who interprets the statement literally will realize that a lot of mediocrity can be sandwiched between good and bad. Item 53 carries an element of sarcasm. Telling a child, "You finally got it" contains the possible hidden message, "It's about time"!

Table 8.1

Ways to Affirm Children's Performance

Superlatives

1. Awesome!
2. Beautiful!
3. Clever!
4. Congratulations!
5. Cool!
6. Dynamite!
7. Exactly!
8. Excellent!
9. Exceptional!
10. Fabulous!
11. Fantastic!
12. Fine!
13. Gorgeous!
14. Great!
15. Incredible!
16. Magnificent!
17. Marvelous!
18. Nice!
19. Outstanding!
20. Sensational!
21. Sharp!
22. Spectacular!
23. Splendid!
24. Super!
25. Superb!
26. Sweet!
27. Swell!
28. Terrific!
29. Tremendous!
30. Wonderful!
31. Wow!
32. Yes!

Specific affirmation: Skill

34. Good job following through.
35. Good move.
36. Good performance.
37. That was right on the money.
38. You're in the groove now.

Specific affirmation: Strategy

39. Good job talking to each other.
40. Now you've figured out a plan.
41. Way to look for a teammate.

Specific affirmation: Attitude

42. Good patience.
43. Good self-control.
44. Thanks for not arguing.

Specific affirmation: Effort

45. Keep it up.
46. One more time and you'll have it.
47. You did a lot of work today.
48. You're really trying hard.
49. You've just about got it.

How not to affirm children

50. Practice makes perfect.
51. That's a good girl.
52. That's not bad.
53. You finally got it.

A leader's role in encouraging children extends to the children themselves. Modeling a variety of ways to give encouragement and directly prodding children can help them to encourage one another. The less experience children have in this role, the more leaders need to reinforce and reward the goal of encouraging peers in a game. Rewards and other postgame responsibilities are discussed in the next section.

Postgame responsibilities

Playing a game can be fun and exciting. In addition to the activity itself, part of the value of a game occurs after it is over. Postgame responsibilities help bring closure to the game experience. Children need closure to reinforce learning and as a transition before they move on to their next endeavor. Specific responsibilities following a game may include returning equipment, discussing the activity, and, for certain special events, giving rewards.

Returning Equipment

Returning equipment usually occurs during the transition between game stoppage and discussion. Often children's excitement and emotions run high at this time. They may be thinking about a controversial rule or a play that was just made. An extra adult may assume responsibility for returning equipment, so the game leader can be free to monitor groups as they sit down together or separately. If an extra adult is not available, student leaders may return equipment, as long as directions are clear, and they finish in time to join the closing discussion.

Discussing Activity

Discussing a game following activity can help achieve at least three purposes. First of all, discussion can help children more fully understand a game. If a child misunderstands a particular rule or strategy, the problem is best cleared up right away, rather than the next time the game is played.

Secondly, discussion helps reinforce the goals of a game. Leaving children with a key principle concerning skills or values provides the best chance that children will apply the same principle in another setting. If a problem occurs during a game, such as players cheating, discussion should not wait until the end of the game. Instead, the leader can stress the importance of honesty for the remainder of the game, without singling out a particular child.

A third purpose of discussing a game is to boost the self-esteem of players. Children who think they did poorly need to hear the leader remind the group that each child is different and trying one's best is the most that can be expected.

Discussion should not be long and drawn out. In fact, a long discussion runs counter to the main purpose of playing a game--to be active. The leader may choose to focus on one of the purposes above, and emphasize a different purpose on another occasion. Over time, all three purposes may be achieved collectively.

Rewarding Children

Rewarding children for their accomplishments communicates that their activities are important and that leaders care about their performance. Certainly God rewards people when they are obedient, although His rewards are often intangible. While we want to reward children tangibly at times, we also need to structure rewards to avoid the following possible shortcomings:

Rewards may be distributed unevenly.

If a lot of emphasis is placed on rewards, and one team seldom earns rewards, they may quit trying. Changing the make-up of teams can help insure that all children earn some rewards, but other shortcomings still warrant consideration.

Rewards may be given too frequently.

Children who receive rewards often may become too extrinsically motivated. They may lose interest in working toward a goal unless a reward is given. Intrinsic motivation can be enhanced by giving rewards some of the time, and other times simply emphasizing that learning is fun and it pleases God. Over time, rewards can be given less often and still be motivating.

Rewards may be esteemed too highly.

Children have a difficult time separating performance from personhood. Their self-esteems can be influenced markedly by performance. Varying the criteria for giving rewards helps all children to succeed. Criteria can help reinforce the importance of what occurs during a game, as well as the outcome of a game. It is inconsistent to tell children the goals of a game are to play hard and have fun, yet reward the "winners." Alternative criteria for rewards include:

    a. Abiding by game rules.
    b. Playing a game safely.
    c. Saying encouraging comments to teammates.

If leaders still wish to occasionally reward the outcome of a game, rewards need not compare one team to another. Additional criteria include:

    d. Having larger team attendance than the previous day.
    e. Scoring more team points than the previous day.
    f. Scoring more combined points (for all teams) than the previous day.

Using inclusive criteria like those suggested has implications for leaders who plan and distribute rewards. Since more children would potentially meet the criteria, more money would be spent on rewards, and more rewards would need to be available on a given day or night.

Closing

"Games for Success" is written to encourage leaders to carefully choose the games children play. The nature of a game is described to emphasize specific elements that may be modified to make games age appropriate, yet flexible, so children of different ability levels may enjoy a high level of success. The book also gives recommendations for developing a healthy self-esteem among children by distinguishing between their personhood and their performance, and by monitoring the conditions under which children are expected to compete.

An important thrust of the book involves integrating biblical values into games so that, over time, leaders may help children refine their character to be more like Christ's. Many games are included so leaders may select activities that have worked in other settings before. While I anticipate leaders utilizing many of these games, my hope and prayer is that leaders--and children themselves--will develop new games using the same principles. And when you do, pass them along to others!

BIBLIOGRAPHY

Ames, C. (1984). Achievement attributions and self-instructions under competitive and individualistic goal structures. *Journal of Educational Psychology, 76* (3), 478-487.

Baumgarten, S. (1988). Nothing short of a revolution. *Journal of Physical Education, Recreation and Dance, 59* (2), 38-41.

Bavolek, S. (1993). *Child centered coaching parent handbook: Having fun and feeling good about me.* Park City, UT: Family Nurturing Center.

Bredemeier, B., & Shields, D. (1984). Divergence in moral reasoning about sport and everyday life. *Sociology of Sport Journal, 1*, 348-357.

Bredemeier, B., & Shields, D. (1986). Game reasoning and interactional morality. *Journal of Genetic Psychology, 147*, 257-275.

Brown, L., & Grineski, S. (1992). Competition in physical education: An educational contradiction? *Journal of Physical Education, Recreation and Dance, 63* (1), 17-19.

Coakley, J. (1990). *Sport in society: Issues and controversies.* St. Louis: Times Mirror/Mosby.

Deline, J. (1991). Why...can't they get along? *Journal of Physical Education, Recreation and Dance, 62* (1), 21-26.

Dobson, J. (1974). *Hide or seek: Self-esteem for the child.* Old Tappan, NJ: Fleming H. Revell.

Duda, R. (1981). *A cross-cultural analysis of achievement motivation in sport and the classroom.* Unpublished doctoral dissertation, University of Illinois, Champaign-Urbana.

Dweck, C., & Elliott, E. (1984). Achievement motivation. In M. Hetherington (Ed.), *Social development: Carmichael's manual of child psychology,* 643-691. New York: Wiley.

Glover, D., & Midura, D. (1992). *Team building through physical challenges.* Champaign, IL: Human Kinetics.

Gould, D. (1984). Psychosocial development and children's sport. In J.R. Thomas (Ed.), *Motor development during childhood and adolescence,* Chapter 11. Minneapolis: Burgess.

Hellison, D. (1987). The affective domain in physical education--Let's do some housecleaning. *Journal of Physical Education, Recreation and Dance,* 58 (6), 41-43.

Huizinga, J. (1955). *Homo ludens: A study of the play element in culture.* Boston: Beacon.

Johnson, D., & Johnson, R. (1974). Instructional goal structure: Cooperative, competitive, or individualistic. *Review of Educational Research,* 44, 213-240.

Johnson, D., & Maruyama, G. et al. (1981). Effects of cooperative, competitive, and individualistic goal structures on achievement: A meta-analysis. *Psychological Bulletin,* 89 (1), 47-62.

Kohn, A. (1992). *No contest: The case against competition.* New York: Houghton Mifflin.

Lentz, T., & Cornelius, R. (1950). *All together: A manual of cooperative games.* St. Louis, MO: Peace Research Laboratory.

Martens, R. (1978). *Joy and sadness in children's sports.* Champaign, IL: Human Kinetics.

Mauldon, E., & Redfern, H. (1981). *Games teaching: An approach to the primary school.* London: MacDonald & Evans.

McDowell, J. (1984). *His image, my image.* San Bernardino, CA: Here's Life Publishers.

Morris, G. (1980). *How to change the games children play* (2nd ed.). Minneapolis: Burgess.

Morris, G., & Stiehl, J. (1989). *Changing kids games.* Champaign, IL: Human Kinetics.

O'Brian, M. (1987). *Vince: A personal biography of Vince Lombardi.* New York: Morrow and Company, Inc.

Orlick, T. (1978). *Winning through cooperation: Competitive insanity, cooperative alternatives.* Washington, D.C.: Acropolis.

Orlick, T. (1981). Positive socialization via cooperative games. *Developmental Psychology,* 17 (4), 426-429.

Orlick, T. (1982). *The second cooperative sports and games book*. New York: Pantheon.

Pangrazi, R. (1982). Physical education, self-concept, and achievement. *Journal of Physical Education, Recreation and Dance, 53* (9), 16-18.

Rainey, D., & Rainey, B. (1986). *Building your mate's self-esteem*. San Barnardino, CA: Here's Life Publishers.

Robinson, D. (1989). An attribution analysis of student demoralization in the physical education setting. *Journal of Educational Psychology, 55,* 27-36.

Ruben, H. (1981). *Competing*. New York: Pinnacle.

Thorpe, R., & Bunker, D. (1986). *Rethinking games teaching*. Loughborough: University of Technology.

Tutko, T., & Bruns, W. (1976). *Winning is everything and other American myths*. New York: Macmillan.

Walker, S. (1980). *Winning: The psychology of competition*. New York: Norton.

Walsh, S. (1987, February 6). Comment: Karate class teaches parent the importance of sports. *The Gateway*, p.2.

Werner, P. (1989). Teaching games: A tactical perspective. *Journal of Physical Education, Recreation and Dance, 60* (3), 97-101.

Wessinger, N. (1994). "I hit a home run!" The lived meaning of scoring in games in physical education. *Quest, 46* (4), 425-439.

Wilson, N. (1976). *The frequency and patterns of utilization of selected motor skills by third and fourth grade girls and boys in the game of kickball*. Unpublished master's project, University of Georgia.

INDEX

Authors

Games *

Biblical

Large Group

* Games followed by an asterisk originated in a country outside the continental United States.

Games

Movements

Movements

About the Author

Steven Henkel received his Bachelor of Science, Master of Science and Doctor of Philosophy degrees in Physical Education at the University of Wisconsin-Madison. He taught physical education four years in the public school, and five years at the University of Wisconsin-Madison while in graduate school.

Steven is currently beginning his 10th year teaching at Bethel College in Saint Paul, Minnesota. He oversees the teacher certification program within the Department of Physical Education, and teaches graduate courses on classroom management and multicultural education. He also leads games in a local church for the AWANA and Vacation Bible School programs, and provides resources to Christian Home Educators. Steven lives with his wife and three sons in Arden Hills, Minnesota.